Literary Lives

General Editor: **Richard Dutton**, Professor of English, Lancaster University

This series offers stimulating accounts of the literary careers of the most admired and influential English-language authors. Volumes follow the outline of the writers' working lives, not in the spirit of traditional biography, but aiming to trace the professional, publishing and social contexts which shaped their writing.

Published titles include:

Cedric C. Brown
JOHN MILTON

Peter Davison
GEORGE ORWELL

Richard Dutton
WILLIAM SHAKESPEARE

Caroline Franklin
BYRON

Kenneth Graham
HENRY JAMES

Lisa Hopkins
CHRISTOPHER MARLOWE

Mary Lago
E. M. FORSTER

Clinton Machann
MATTHEW ARNOLD

Kerry McSweeney
GEORGE ELIOT

Gerald Roberts
GERARD MANLEY HOPKINS

Felicity Rosslyn
ALEXANDER POPE

Tony Sharpe
T. S. ELIOT
WALLACE STEVENS

Peter Shillingsburg
WILLIAM MAKEPEACE THACKERAY

Grahame Smith
CHARLES DICKENS

Janice Farrar Thaddeus
FRANCES BURNEY

Linda Wagner-Martin
SYLVIA PLATH

Nancy A. Walker
KATE CHOPIN

John Williams
MARY SHELLEY
WILLIAM WORDSWORTH

Tom Winnifrith and Edward Chitham
CHARLOTTE AND EMILY BRONTË

John Worthen
D. H. LAWRENCE

David Wykes
EVELYN WAUGH

Literary Lives
Series Standing Order ISBN 0–333–71486–5 hardcover
Series Standing Order ISBN 0–333–80334–5 paperback
(*outside North America only*)

You can receive future titles in thi ⋯ der.
Please contact your bookseller or, ⋯ ith
your name and address, the title c ⋯

Customer Services Department, ⋯ ⋯ oke,
Hampshire RG21 6XS, England

Rhythm Arts Journal
(© *the Fergusson Gallery, Perth and Kinross Council, Scotland*).

Katherine Mansfield

A Literary Life

Angela Smith
Professor of English Studies
University of Stirling

First published 2000 by
PALGRAVE
Houndmills, Basingstoke, Hampshire RG21 6XS and
175 Fifth Avenue, New York, N. Y. 10010
Companies and representatives throughout the world

PALGRAVE is the new global academic imprint of
St. Martin's Press LLC Scholarly and Reference Division and
Palgrave Publishers Ltd (formerly Macmillan Press Ltd).

ISBN 0–333–61877–7 hardback
ISBN 0–333–61878–5 paperback

This book is printed on paper suitable for recycling and
made from fully managed and sustained forest sources.

A catalogue record for this book is available
from the British Library.

Library of Congress Cataloging-in-Publication Data
Smith, Angela, 1941–
     Katherine Mansfield—a literary life / Angela Smith.
          p. cm. — (Literary lives)
     Includes bibliographical references and index.
     ISBN 0–333–61877–7
     1. Mansfield, Katherine, 1888–1923. 2. Authors, New Zealand—20th
century—Biography. I. Title. II. Literary lives (New York, N. Y.)
     PR9639.3.M258 Z877 2000
     823'.912—dc21
     [B]
                                                              00-041495

10   9   8   7   6   5   4   3   2   1
09   08   07   06   05   04   03   02   01   00

Printed and bound in Great Britain by
Antony Rowe Ltd, Chippenham, Wiltshire

For Helena Smith, and in loving memory of the women in our family who were Mansfield's contemporaries – Mollie Hookham, Nancy Poulter, Lil Huggett, Grace Harbott and May Poulter.

Contents

Acknowledgements

I have been helped more than they know by a group of colleagues at the University of Stirling whose scholarly interest in Modernism has informed my work, and whose imaginative engagement with the arts of the early years of the twentieth century has opened up new perspectives for me. They are Rory Watson, Grahame Smith and Otto Karolyi in English Studies; Nick Royle, formerly in English Studies; Helen Beale in the French Department; and Valerie Fairweather in the Library. Gordon Willis in the University Library has been tirelessly helpful and efficient in tracking down books and obtaining them quickly. Colleagues and students in the Centre of Commonwealth Studies have provided a congenial atmosphere for discussing my work on Mansfield; I should like to thank specifically John McCracken, Robin Law, Sudesh Mishra, James Procter, Renata Casertano, Maggie Nolan, Jane Stewart and Fiona Chalamanda. I should also like to thank Kirsten Simister, the curator of the Fergusson Gallery in Perth, for her help, and for allowing me access to Fergusson's sketchbooks. Bruce Bennett and Adrian Caesar kindly helped me to identify a painting in the Australian War Memorial at Canberra. Jacqueline Bardolph, of the University of Nice, and I shared an unusual common interest in the work of Mansfield and of Ngugi wa Thiong'o; she was a valued friend and colleague. She died in July 1999; I shall miss her vigorous, warm and witty presence, and her scholarship.

The greatest debt of love, as Mansfield calls it, is to my family, and cannot be paid. Matthew's interest in the detail and design of paintings has offered me new ways of seeing. Grahame and Dan have been generous in sharing their knowledge of early twentieth-century cinema and music with me; both have commented in detail on drafts of this book, and I am grateful for their thoughtfulness and insight.

The author wishes to thank the following copyright holders for permission to use material:

Alfred A. Knopf, a division of Random House Inc, for extracts from *The Short Stories of Katherine Mansfield*. Copyright 1937 and renewed 1965 by Alfred A. Knopf, Inc.

Oxford University Press for extracts from *The Collected Letters of Katherine Mansfield*, 4 vols (Oxford: Clarendon Press, 1984–96).

Margaret Scott and Daphne Brasell Associates for extracts from *The Katherine Mansfield Notebooks* (NZ: Lincoln University Press and Daphne Brasell Associates, 1997).

The Fergusson Gallery, Perth and Kinross Council, for permission to reproduce the cover of *Rhythm*.

1
Introduction

I live to write.[1]

The first entry in *The Katherine Mansfield Notebooks* is 'Enna Blake', a story that she wrote when she was nine; it was published in *The High School Reporter* in Wellington, New Zealand, accompanied by the schoolgirl editor's comment that it 'shows promise of great merit'.[2] This first story is set in Britain, before Mansfield had been there; like so much of Mansfield's later fiction, it begins with a train journey, and pivots on plants. When Enna, a ten-year-old, arrives at her destination, Torquay, 'Mrs Brown proposed that they should go ferning'.[3] The gap between the metropolitan and colonial cultures opens; little girls in Torquay go primrosing or blackberrying, not ferning. Tracing the literary consequences as Mansfield negotiates, and eventually celebrates, that gap is an underlying preoccupation in her writing; Angela Carter defines Mansfield 'as unforgiven prodigal daughter to Britain, a culture of which she was subtly never a part'.[4]

Mansfield lived in Britain, the Mediterranean and Switzerland, from 1908 until her death early in 1923, during what Carter rather provocatively calls England's last artistically vital period. For most of that time she was actively involved in the literary life of London, as a contributor to little magazines and as a reviewer for various journals including the *Athenaeum* when her husband, John Middleton Murry, was its editor. The world of letters was as exclusive as the society of which it was a part. Two anecdotes from well-connected British writers of the period hint at an unthinking imperial snobbery directed towards the 'little colonial', as Mansfield called

1

and sensitively showy bad taste'.[7] A glance at photographs of
Ottoline Morrell, apparently habitually dressed for a part as a pan-
tomime dame, and a source for D. H. Lawrence's Hermione Roddice
in *Women in Love*, makes this a particularly startling allegation, but
it perhaps in itself suggests the hegemonic view that could so unself-
consciously construct the colonial foreigner as childlike and inferior.
Morrell says she thought of Mansfield 'as taking her brother – and
later on taking Murry – by the hand and scampering off into this
imaginary world of adventure – enchanting, gay and unscrupulous –
for certainly she and Murry carried out many an escapade that did
not fit in with our ordinary code'.[8] That code accommodated what,
by Mansfield's possibly more sensitive provincial standards, included
habitual emotional betrayal, but was authorized by imperial and
class status.

Modernism in literature in English is of course dominated by non-
British writers, notably Conrad, Joyce and T. S. Eliot. Mansfield was
not unique in being an outsider, but she was also hampered in her
ambition to write by her gender and her illness. This will be explored
in subsequent chapters, but it is relevant to her reputation among
writers who were her contemporaries. She was ill for so long that
other writers seem to have suspected her of making literary capital
out of it. D. H. Lawrence wrote to their mutual friend, Koteliansky, in
1921 that Murry is 'on the Riviera with K[atherine] – who is doing
the last gasp touch, in order to impose on people … Two mud-worms
they are, playing into each other's long mud-bellies'.[9] Other writers,
jealous of her growing reputation and suspicious of antipodean
tricks, were similarly sceptical, and even posthumous myths about
her hampered assessments of her writing. Murry's daughter, the child
of the second of his four marriages, describes the iconic status that
he accorded his dead first wife:

> Katherine would live on by the very fact of his own living love
> for her. He would not let her die. Her presence would accompany
> him always.
>
> The altar was now draped for the Katherine Mansfield cult; the
> French threw themselves [*sic*] into it with even greater gusto than
> the English. About my own youthful nostrils floated the per-
> fumed incense of genius, sweet and sickly, indescribable, unnam-
> able [*sic*], invisible, and yet for ever there.[10]

The painter Carrington wrote to Gerald Brennan after Mansfield's death with a similar interpretation of events, affirming that Mansfield was 'very much a female of the underworld, with the language of a fishwife in Wapping. Murry's circle in Hampstead is now making her into a mystical Keats.'[11]

This macabre sanctification was effected through Murry's power as an editor. At the time of her death, Mansfield had published only three volumes of stories: *In a German Pension* (1911), *Bliss and Other Stories* (1920) and *The Garden Party and Other Stories* (1922). She left all her papers to her husband, with a letter asking him to 'Go through them one day, dear love, and destroy all you do not use. Please destroy all letters you do not wish to keep and all papers. You know my love of tidiness. Have a clean sweep, Bogey, and leave all fair – will you?'[12] What Murry inherited were 53 notebooks and hundreds of loose pages of Mansfield's appallingly difficult handwriting. Margaret Scott, who has definitively released Mansfield from Murry's versions of her by producing an edition of all the extant notebooks and papers, and, with Vincent O'Sullivan, of her letters,[13] speculates that she is unlikely to have carted them all about with her on her travels in search of a congenial climate, and may have lodged them with the London branch of the Bank of New Zealand, of which her father was chairman. In the year of her death, Murry's first trawl of the papers resulted in *Poems by Katherine Mansfield* and a collection of stories, *The Dove's Nest*. In the following year, another posthumous volume of stories appeared, *Something Childish and Other Stories*. The creation of a persona for his dead wife was effected through his selection of material from the notebooks and papers over the next few years. The first volume of extracts, *The Journal of Katherine Mansfield*, was published in 1927; it was so popular that Murry then published *The Scrapbook of Katherine Mansfield* in 1939, 'thus creating the impression that KM had kept two books to write in – one a journal and the other a scrapbook'.[14] In 1954 the *Journal of Katherine Mansfield: Definitive Edition* was produced, with an editorial preface explaining that

> passages have been restored which for various reasons were suppressed in the original edition of 1927. Other passages have been incorporated which, though actually published in the *Scrapbook* in 1939, really belong to the *Journal* and would have been included in it, if they had been discovered in time.[15]

A two-volume edition of Mansfield's letters appeared in 1928, edited by Murry; in 1951 he published *Katherine Mansfield's Letters to John Middleton Murry*.

Murry's control over the production of the Mansfield myth can be compared to the editorial function exercised by Leonard Woolf and by Ted Hughes in relation to their dead wives' personal writings.[16] Murry's reasons for creating the sanitized version of Mansfield that first appeared are complex: the quantities of barely legible handwriting must have been daunting; the feelings of living family and acquaintances had to be considered; the full revelation of her loneliness and suffering often cast him, whatever the reality of the situation, in the role of insensitive egoist. He may have had in mind her warning to him in a letter of July 1917, motivated by her wariness of the predatory literary world she felt they inhabited: 'dont lower your mask until you have another mask prepared beneath – As terrible as you like – but a *mask*'.[17] The initial mask that he created for her was that of Brooke's 'lidy', removing the vitriol and wit as well as despair from Mansfield's personal writing. The effect of having access to the full range of the notebooks, and to as many letters as are known to exist, is to enable the reader to recognize the bravery with which Mansfield confronted her tragic illness and early death, but also to see that courage constantly contextualized by her obsessive preoccupation with writing. Her record of her first death warrant, as she was well aware that Keats called it, shows her priorities:

> I spat – it tasted strange – it was bright red blood. Since then Ive gone on spitting each time I cough a little more. Oh, yes, of course I am frightened. But for two reasons only ... I shan't have my work written. Thats what matters. How unbearable it would be to die, to leave 'scraps', 'bits', nothing really finished. but I feel the first thing to do is to get back to Jack.[18]

Mansfield's life and protracted death were dominated by her writing. As Margaret Scott remarks, it is often difficult to tell from the *Notebooks* whether Mansfield is writing of actual or imagined events. The tendency of a lot of criticism of her fiction is to read it as autobiographical because, like Sylvia Plath's, the narrative of the life is compelling. As Ted Hughes was in relation to Plath, Murry has been demonized by critics of Mansfield's work; Vincent O'Sullivan remarks that criticism of him,

> often reads as though the commentator were obliged to live with him, and so finds him wanting on scores whose relevance is not always obvious. As literary history stands at the moment, Murry has had what may be the worst press of any writer among his contemporaries, apart from Aleister Crowley.[19]

Murry's self-justifying attempts to defend himself, such as his autobiography *Between Two Worlds* (1935), were a much less effective response to his situation than Hughes's *Birthday Letters*, but this book will not read Mansfield's fiction or Murry's writing in order to make deductions about her relationship with Murry, or with her family. It will concentrate on the literary and artistic context within which Mansfield created her fiction, focusing on her position as an outsider in British life, with experience of the conflict between Maori and pakeha cultures in New Zealand; throughout I use 'pakeha', the Maori term for 'white', as it is used in New Zealand. It will consider the intellectual and imaginative stimulus she gained from meeting writers and reviewing, but will focus particularly on her involvement with the visual arts, an element in her development that is commented on but not explored, either in literary criticism or in the major biographies, Antony Alpers' *The Life of Katherine Mansfield* and Claire Tomalin's *Katherine Mansfield: A Secret Life*.

Mansfield's first extant letter, written from London to a schoolfriend in Wellington, is about the art of the imperial capital, in Westminster Abbey, St Paul's and the British Museum: 'enough Julius Caesar's to last you a lifetime, with noses, and minus noses'. She describes sculpture as 'a huge revelation' because of 'the indescribable beauty of form and attitude, that can be hewn out of a block of marble'. She is also deeply impressed by Watts' paintings in the Tate because the 'most marvellous originality of colour is so striking, the depth of his reds, the calm peace of his blues'.[20] At 14, she is already preoccupied by form and colour rather than, for instance, narrative interpretation of Watts' allegorical paintings. Some of her most revealing letters about writing were penned, not for other authors, but for painters; for instance, she expects, rightly, that Dorothy Brett will engage with her in trying to analyse form in painting and writing. As well as Brett, her other closest female friends were painters: Beatrice Campbell and Anne Estelle Rice, the American painter who, when Mansfield first knew her, was close to the Scottish Colourist, J. D. Fergusson. Fergusson himself is one of the few friends and contemporaries about whom Mansfield is consistently loving and admiring in her personal writing; she tells Ida Baker in 1918:

> Johnny came in last night – God! – He gave me such a welcome. Before I knew where I was we had hugged & kissed each other & Johnny kept saying 'this is a great success'. It really was! And you can imagine all the enjoyment he got out of a *fig* or two. We are dining with him tonight.[21]

The significance of Mansfield's friendship with Fergusson, and his group of painters, will be developed more fully in Chapters 4 and 5; it is relevant to Mansfield's uneasy relationship with the Bloomsbury coterie in her position as a New Zealander. Leonard and Virginia Woolf, when the Hogarth Press published 'Prelude', used the woodcuts that Fergusson made for the cover on only a few copies because they disliked them; this in miniature reflects a more significant exclusion. Mansfield writes about it to Murry when she tells him that Virginia 'dislikes the [Fergusson] drawings very much. So does Leonard. Well, they would – wouldn't they?…Ill send you her letter, however – & Ill write to her & ask her to send you a proof of the cover – I don't want Roger Fly on it, at any rate'.[22] She mocks the eminent art critic and painter, a close friend of his biographer Virginia Woolf, by reducing him to an insect because she recognizes his power to marginalize, a comparable experience to that of the 'little colonial'. In her history of British art since 1900, Frances Spalding remarks of the Scottish Colourists, Fergusson, Cadell, Peploe and Hunter:

> Fergusson was the first to adopt Matisse's rich colour which, with an abbreviated method of drawing, came to distinguish their art. 'Paris is simply a place of freedom,' he later recalled. 'It allowed me to be Scots as I understand it.' Despite the importance of these four artists, none was included in Roger Fry's Second Post-Impressionist Exhibition of 1912, an omission that reflects on the English tendency to relegate Scottish art to a secondary, peripheral position.[23]

Anna Greutzner Robins makes a similar point: 'Many critics thought that J. D. Fergusson and Anne Estelle Rice and their group should have been included in the *Second Post-Impressionist Exhibition.*'[24] The affinity between Mansfield and Fergusson in their social position in the English art world is mirrored in their colourism; Mansfield sees as Fergusson paints. Scenes from Mansfield's letters and notebooks are often framed for their recipient, usually Murry, presented as a Fauvist painting, with clearly outlined squares and rectangles, a dense use of colour, no perspective, and no shadows:

> My small, pale yellow house with a mimosa tree growing in front of it – just a bit deeper yellow – the garden, full of plants, the terrace with crumbling yellow pillars covered with green (lurking-place for lizards) all belong to a picture or a story – I mean they are not remote from one's ideal – one's dream. The house faces the sea, but to the right there is the Old Town with a small harbour, a little quai planted with pepper and plane trees. This Old Town, which is built flat against a hill – a solid wall, as it were, of shapes & colours is the finest thing Ive seen.[25]

The phrase 'one's ideal – one's dream' signals Mansfield's artistic alignment which derives from her early association with Fergusson and the *Rhythm* group; it suggests an essential link between the surface and the profound self which preoccupies Post-Impressionist painters.

Mansfield's writing is sometimes described as Impressionist rather than Post-Impressionist. Vincent O'Sullivan considers that 'Mansfield's early enthusiasm for Pater had taken her directly to the beginnings of European Impressionism, and to that sense of isolation that is at its centre';[26] Kate Fullbrook agrees:

> An impressionistic impulse is behind 'Prelude'; the characters are presented in terms of the intersection of light and shade … Identity in the story is as impermanent as the dappled moments in a Renoir or a Manet, and the temporary look of things – people, objects, social relations – is all that the narrative claims to know with any certainty.[27]

Sarah Sandley, who idiosyncratically classifies Cézanne as an Impressionist rather than a Post-Impressionist, writes: 'Mansfield strikes many as a Literary Impressionist, for whom the focus is, as Julia van Gunsteren describes it, "on perception … This fragmentary, momentary, evocative reality *is* or *becomes* reality for the Literary

Impressionist."'[28] Hanson and Gurr, however, suggest that Mansfield's writing 'can more usefully and accurately be compared to Post-Impressionist rather than to Impressionist painting, for we need more emphasis on the solidity of the structure of her stories and on their weight of implication. In this Cézanne, whom she admired, is a better parallel than Renoir, whom she did not'.[29] Mansfield's comment on Renoir's painting, in a letter to Brett, clarifies her rejection of surface realism, in his painting and by implication in her own writing:

> Renoir – at the last – bores me. His feeling for flesh is a kind of super butchers feeling about a lovely little cut of lamb. I am always fascinated by lovely bosoms but not without the heads & hands as well – and I want in fact the feeling that all this beauty is in the deepest sense attached to Life.[30]

The distinction between the two movements is a crucial one for understanding Mansfield's intellectual and artistic milieu. Wallace Martin comments on landmarks in British cultural life in the first two decades of the twentieth century that led to significant changes: the influence of Bergson's philosophy; the appearance of the first of Freud's books to be published in Britain, *The Interpretation of Dreams*; the impact of the two Post-Impressionist exhibitions which included Van Gogh's Expressionist paintings; the appearance of the Russian ballet with sets by Bakst and music by Stravinsky; the publication of translations of Russian fiction, particularly of works by Chekhov. He charts the changes in the group that were writing for the *New Age* at the time when it included Mansfield and her mentor, A. R. Orage:

> Between 1911 and 1914, it absorbed a number of new cultural forces and became the haven of the new writers and artists who emerged just before the war. The new contributors were, on the whole, individualist rather than collectivist; they displayed little interest in the political, social, and economic ideas that had animated their predecessors; artistically, they were expressionists rather than impressionists.[31]

Mansfield was permitted by her reluctant father, after a sustained campaign on her part, to return from New Zealand to London in July 1908; having got what she wanted, she entered vigorously, through her involvement with Orage and the *New Age*, into an intellectual and cultural life that was in ferment. Particular aspects of literary and artistic innovation will be discussed as they occur chronologically, but a general understanding of her context requires an exploration of the crucial differences between Impressionism and the strand of Post-Impressionism that most influenced Mansfield, Fauvism, and of the role of the philosopher Henri Bergson in its innovations. Bergson was a major intellectual influence on Fergusson and Murry at the time that they met in Paris in 1911, and their excitement about his ideas was communicated to Mansfield when she was introduced to Murry in December of the following year, as is evident in her contributions to editorials for *Rhythm*.

Bergson's exploration of intuition in *Time and Free Will* (1889, first English version 1910) suggests that we have two selves, one which we reach 'by deep introspection, which leads us to grasp our inner states as living things, constantly *becoming*, as states not amenable to measure, which permeate one another' and another where 'we live outside ourselves, hardly perceiving anything of ourselves but our own ghost ... we live for the external world rather than for ourselves; we speak rather than think; we "are acted" rather than act ourselves. To act freely is to recover possession of oneself'.[32] In *Inventing Bergson*, Mark Antliff interprets Impressionism as being expressive of the second state, of the external world, grasping surfaces rather than psychological depths: 'emotions and deep structures were antithetical to Impressionism'.[33] Bergson's argument is that living for the external world is a kind of automatism, which overcomes freedom in those who 'are fond of setting psychic states side by side, of forming a chain or a line of them', with each part of the sequence having a separate and homogeneous identity which is false to the merging and becoming process of psychic states. This conceptualization involves an idea of space, of taking a position outside consciousness to codify it, whereas if there is no idea of space, consciousness's sensations

> will add themselves dynamically to one another and will organize themselves, like the successive tones of a tune by which we allow ourselves to be lulled and soothed. In a word, pure duration might well be nothing but a succession of qualitative changes, which melt into and permeate one another, without precise outlines,

without any tendency to externalize themselves in relation to one another, without any affiliation with number: it would be pure heterogeneity.[34]

The representation of this heterogeneity in painting or writing is problematic: 'all forms of self-representation would seem self-defeating – inevitably the profound self is refracted and impoverished through the very mechanism of self-representation'.[35] However, if the artist avoids linear sequentiality, he or she may, by a juxtaposition of images, be able to elicit in the observer an intuitive response to the artist's deep self. Single images offer only sequentiality and a spatial experience, at odds with the 'duration' in which melting and permeating take place:

> No image will replace the intuition of the duration, but many different images, taken from quite different orders of things, will be able, through the convergence of their action, to direct consciousness to the precise point where there is a certain intuition to seize on. By choosing images as dissimilar as possible, any one of them will be prevented from usurping the place of the intuition it is instructed to call forth.[36]

To give a simplified example, Monet's sequence paintings could be seen as individually homogeneous, in that they show haystacks or Rouen cathedral in particular lights and moods, whereas Robert Delaunay's Cubist *Eiffel Tower* (1911), painted from memory, gives a multiplicity of angles, a heterogeneity, what Antliff describes as 'an intuitive amalgam of the public's thoughts about this icon of modernism'.[37] Impressionism privileges surface appearances and the viewer's eye, whereas Post-Impressionism, and literary modernism in at least some of its manifestations, are concerned with the profound self, and with deep structures. A literary equivalent of the Monet/Delaunay analogy might be a comparison between Dowson's city poems and T. S. Eliot's 'The Love Song of J. Alfred Prufrock', one of Mansfield's favourite works. 'Prufrock' piles up dissonant images and moods, crabs on the sea-floor and society ladies in drawing rooms, cats and mermaids, requiring an intuitive and imaginative response from the reader to the profound self revealed, consciously or not, by the speaker.

J. D. Fergusson did not become a Cubist painter like Delaunay, but he was intrigued by the experimental painting he encountered in Paris when he moved there from Scotland in 1907. He writes of his antipathy to traditional portraiture, and so

> when in Paris I saw Picasso's portrait of a woman with a guitar in the rue Vignon on an Opening Day in 1907, I was not surprised to find progressions of forms contained, or not, by lines in har- monisation of planes – a complexity of forms instead of the Beaux Arts smoothness.[38]

A self-taught artist, Fergusson found in Paris the artistic and social stimulus that he was looking for; in the cafés 'the great attraction was the girl frequenters. They were chiefly girls employed by dress- makers and milliners and wore things they were working at, mostly too extreme from a practical point of view, but with that touch of daring that made them very helpful'.[39] What Fergusson was devel- oping was a Fauvist aesthetic; he felt at home with the dressmakers and milliners in the café he frequented because they were not preoc- cupied by respectability, and were 'natural'; 'these charming girls' were 'quite pleased to be drawn and didn't become self-conscious or take frozen poses'.[40] This was no longer the world of Whistler's soci- ety portraits and muted grey land and river scapes, which influ- enced Fergusson earlier in his career. The Paris Fauves (wild beasts) were Matisse, Derain and Vlaminck; their work was characterized by a sensuous and heightened use of colour, especially red and green, an emphatic outlining of figures, and an interest in 'primitive' sub- jects. The link between Fauvism and Bergson's philosophy is reiter- ated in *Rhythm*, the magazine initiated by John Middleton Murry with Fergusson as art editor in 1911:

> Modernism is not the capricious outburst of intellectual dipsoma- nia. It penetrates beneath the outward surface of the world, and disengages the rhythms that lie at the heart of things, rhythms strange to the eye, unaccustomed to the ear, primitive harmonies of the world that is and lives.[41]

There is a transgressive impetus to all the forms of art that are pre- sented or reviewed in the magazine, in keeping with the sense of social exclusion felt by Fergusson as a Scot and Mansfield as a New Zealander; these arts are admired for their capacity to reveal the strange, the barbaric. In an issue that contains Mansfield's story 'The Woman at the Store', her most overtly disorientating story,[42] Michael Sadler has a piece entitled 'After Gauguin' in which he writes: 'An art intent on expressing the *inner* soul of persons and things will inevitably stray from the *outer* conventions of form and colour; that is to say, it will be definitely unnaturalistic, anti-materialist.'[43]

Fergusson's painting will be discussed in more detail in relation to Mansfield's writing in a subsequent chapter, but their shared enthusiasm for Bergson's ideas needs to be understood as a rejection both of the surface realism of Impressionism and of art as realistic social criticism. She comments in her notebook on art's ability to heighten and distort, as the Fauvists did:

> reality cannot become the ideal, the dream, and it is not the business of the artist to grind an axe, to try and impose his vision of Life upon the existing world. Art is not an attempt to reconcile existence with his vision: it is an attempt to create his own world *in* this world. That which suggests the subject to the artist is the unlikeness of it to what we accept as reality. We single out, we bring into the light, we put up higher.[44]

The poet René Arcos, also deeply influenced by Bergson, describes a painter's stroll from his house: 'Instead of throwing fleeting glances at things in the course of habitual activity, the perceptually gifted artist "lingers on objects" and continually "discovers them" anew.'[45] Both writer and painter discover mundane things by singling them out, 'putting them up higher', revealing vital similarities and rhythms. Fergusson's description of how he came to paint his picture called *Rose Rhythm* and Mansfield's letter to him about the painting signal how well she intuits what he is attempting. At a time when he and Mansfield were living in the same street in London, in 1914, a dancer called Kathleen Dillon came to visit Fergusson and his wife:

> One day she arrived with a remarkable hat. I said, 'that's a very good hat you've got.' She said, 'Yes! isn't it? I've just made it.' It was just like a rose, going from the central convolution and continuing the 'Rhythm' idea developed in Paris and still with me. Looking at K I soon saw that the hat was not merely a hat, but a continuation of the girl's character, her mouth, her nostril, the curl of her hair – her whole character…I painted 'Rose Rhythm' – going

from the very central convolutions to her nostril, lips, eyebrows, brooch, buttons, background cushions, right through.[46]

Mansfield, writing to Fergusson four years after he painted the picture, remembers it:

> I have a vase of roses and buds before me on the table. I had a good *look* at them last night and your rose picture was vivid before me – I saw it in every curve of these beauties – the blouse like a great petal, the round brooch, the rings of hair like shavings of light. I thought how supremely you had 'brought it off'.[47]

The repeated heart shapes in the painting, the patterned suggestion that the subject is flowering and that the flowers are feminine, vigorous rather than decorative, have elicited the intuitive recognition in Mansfield that Bergson requires of dynamic art.

The fact that Mansfield and Murry were known as the Tigers suggests their identification with the wildness of Fauvism. Accounts of Fergusson's studio and Mansfield's many writing rooms sometimes resemble Fauvist interiors. Mansfield herself describes visiting Fergusson in what might be an interior by Matisse, with geometric shapes, no shadows, clear outlines, a heightened palette and distorted light, as it is both sunny and raining:

> The sun came full through the two windows, dividing the studio into four – two quarters of light and two of shadow. But all those things which the light touched seemed to float in it, to bathe and to sparkle in it as if they belonged not to land but to water; they even seemed, in some strange way, to be moving... Very beautiful, oh God is a blue teapot with two white cups attending, a red apple among oranges addeth fire to flame – in the white bookcases the books fly up and down in scales of colour, with pink and lilac notes recurring... White net curtains hang over the windows. For all the sun it is raining outside.[48]

This colourist description is comparable with William Orton's account of 'Catherine's' rooms in *The Last Romantic*, in which Mansfield creates a *mise en scène* for herself:

> She had made the place look quite beautiful – a couple of candles stuck in a skull, another behind the high windows, a lamp on the

herself: for them her manners, her passion and the success of her stories all betray her dubious origins. The poet Rupert Brooke wrote to Edward Marsh, an influential patron of the arts, in 1913:

> Katherine Tiger [Mansfield] is in the country. She got turned out of an omnibus the other day for calling a woman a whore. She really ought to remember she's a lidy. The provocation was that the woman said that all suffragettes ought to be trampled to death by horses. Katherine tho' not a suffragette protested, and the woman said, 'You with your painted lips!' Rather a squalid little story.[5]

Brooke, who may be mocking Mansfield's accent when he writes 'lidy' and whose use of her nickname is an indication of distaste about voracious women, seems to perceive squalor in Mansfield's outspoken and disinterested defence of suffragettes, and in the fact that she was wearing make-up at the time, rather than in the dreary and vicious stereotypes offered by the woman on the bus. Vulgarity and colonial provenance are presented with an unspoken assumption that they will be linked in the mind of the recipient, as they are in an entry, nearly ten years later, in Virginia Woolf's diary. She records, perhaps with an ironic awareness of her consuming jealousy of Mansfield, that T. S. Eliot is starting a magazine, *The Criterion*, and that she and her husband, Leonard, are to contribute to it:

> So what does it matter if K.M. soars in the newspapers, runs up sales skyhigh? Ah, I have found a fine way of putting her in her place. The more she is praised, the more I am convinced she is bad. After all, there's some truth in this. She touches the spot too universally for that spot to be of the bluest blood.[6]

Popularity is vulgar; Woolf occupies the aesthetic and lineal high ground. Lady Ottoline Morrell, often hostess at her house, Garsington, for the Bloomsbury Group, endorses Woolf's position. She comments, after Mansfield's death, on the fact that 'she was conscious of being a New Zealander, secretly proud of it' as if it were a furtive but alluring vice. She was 'Japanese in appearance, also I should have said in mind – she had their delicate, exotic vulgarity floor shining through yellow chrysanthemums, and herself accurately in the centre, in a patterned pink kimono and white flowered frock, the one cluster of primary brightness in the room. A painting of a river flowing through reedy country was on one wall, a stack of canvases and a bundle of tall dry rushes in a corner, and two crosspieces of a strainer up on a nail looking like a deserted crucifix.[49]

The objects in the room have been isolated to suggest deep structures, the skull indicating Mansfield's abiding preoccupation with death, and the tea strainer hinting at her precarious atheism. Virginia Woolf's report that Mansfield 'liked "to have a line round her"'[50] sounds like a description of a Fauvist painting, and seems also to have applied to Fergusson: 'That his subjects were part and parcel of his own self-image as a Fauve finds no better confirmation than in the studio décor itself.'[51]

Each chapter of this book will include an analysis of a particular story or stories by Mansfield, to exemplify stages of the argument about her shifting and disrupted development as a writer. The introductory chapter has focused on her awareness of her own foreignness in Europe, and on her commitment to a group of Fauvist artists who were also predominantly not English, and who were excluded by the Bloomsbury avant garde. It concludes by considering '*Je ne parle pas français*' as an exploration of what it is to be foreign, suggesting that the story can be read through Fauvist painting. It is not surprising that she sent the story to Fergusson, wanting him to read it, though there is no evidence of whether he did. She writes to Murry that she herself is perplexed by it; she 'couldn't think where the devil I had got the bloody thing from – I cant even now. Its a mystery. Theres so much less taken from life than anybody would credit.'[52] In the same letter she tells him, in terms that suggest the tiger, that she has 'gone for it, bitten deeper & deeper & deeper than ever I have before'. That she is mystified by the story signals its Fauvist impetus: there is a wildness underlying its superficial control, as there is in the narrator, Raoul Duquette. When Mansfield was asked whether she would permit the story to be cut by Michael Sadler for publication by Constable, she replied angrily: 'No, Ill never agree. Ill supply another story but that is all. The *outline* would be all blurred. It must have those sharp lines.'[53] The last comments could have been made of a painting such as *Rhythm* by Fergusson, where the central figure is sharply outlined with an emphatic line, and where the shapes are unexplained; the curving and powerful female figure in the picture has a severely perpendicular line to her left arm and buttocks which contrasts with the sinuous curves elsewhere in the painting. '*Je ne parle pas français*' was first printed for private circulation by the Heron Press in 1919; Murry and his brother Richard did the printing. When the story was published by Constable in *Bliss and Other Stories*, Sadler insisted on the changes to it which Mansfield initially resisted, and then accepted, apparently because she wanted an advance payment from Constable. Significantly, Murry's recommendation in 1920 was distinctly on the side of caution rather than savagery. He thought that people like his mother would read the stories: 'Now these people will be shocked by the few things the omission of which is still suggested. I believe that it's bad policy to shock the people by whom, after all, you do desire to be read.'[54]

'*Je ne parle pas français*' is unusual among Mansfield's stories in that it has a first-person narrator rather than the fluid narrative perspective of such stories as 'Prelude' and 'Bliss'. The plot is clearly delineated, and is quite simple: the narrator's English friend, Dick Harmon, arrives in Paris with a woman who is not his wife, and who is never named. He abandons her without having occupied the hotel rooms he has asked Duquette to book for them, because he feels guilt about having left his mother alone in England. The narrator promises to return to help the deserted woman, who cannot speak French, but does not do so. The story, like a painting, is in a frame. The first and final sections are set in the present, in a Parisian café, and the rest is a memory focusing round the phrase, from the present, '*je ne parle pas français*'. There are 23 sections, varying in length and with the last four becoming distinctly staccato. Each section has its own sharp outline; the story does not waver from one section to another as 'The Daughters of the Late Colonel' does. In this it mirrors its narrator, who is always conscious of his own image: 'I read it standing in front of the (unpaid for) wardrobe mirror. It was early morning. I wore a blue kimono embroidered with white birds and my hair was still wet; it lay on my forehead, wet and gleaming.'[55] The clarity of the visual image is, however, repeatedly undermined by what it suggests, this time to the narrator himself, who sees himself as a picture: '"Portrait of Madame Butterfly," said I, "on hearing of the arrival of *ce cher Pinkerton*"' (74). Duquette's sexual orientation, as with much else about him, remains blurred despite the sharpness of the outline;[56] he seems to be physically stimulated by both Harmon and his female companion, and the implication is that he is both pimp and prostitute, cooperating in being a sexual object for predatory women but transgressive in his own self-image: 'I confess, without my clothes I am rather charming. Plump, almost like a girl, with smooth shoulders, and I wear a thin gold bracelet above my left elbow' (68).

The shape of the sections also hints at frames, though not of paintings; the recurrent motif that Duquette uses is photography. He describes the waiter in the café 'waiting to be photographed in connection with some wretched murder' (62); it begins to seem that the sections of the story are a series of snapshots. He compares himself to a prostitute 'who has to introduce herself with a handful of photographs' (68–9) which are pornographic clichés, 'Me in my chemise, coming out of an eggshell ... Me upside down in a swing' (69). As the story speeds up, the images become more cinematic, though the frames remain separate. When the Englishwoman asks, in a moment of crisis, for tea, Duquette wants to protest because it 'seemed to me so amazingly in the picture' (82). Underlying all these images is the narrator's conviction that life is predictable and conforms to stereotypes. He asks himself early on why he sees life 'as a rag-picker on the American cinema, shuffling along wrapped in a filthy shawl with her old claws crooked over a stick' and replies that this is the 'direct result of the American cinema acting upon a weak mind' (62). The reader is never allowed to forget that the narrator's consciousness is moulded by images from the popular culture of his time; he sees the waiter 'carrying the tea-tray high on one hand as if the cups were cannon-balls and he a heavy-weight lifter on the cinema' (84). He is such an eager audience at the drama opening out before him that he sometimes describes what he sees as if it were happening on the screen, in black and white, visually anticipating the *film noir* of the 1940s, as he does here when Harmon, Duquette and the woman are travelling in a taxi:

I had insisted on taking the flap seat facing them because I would not have missed for anything those occasional flashing glimpses I had as we broke through the white circles of lamplight.

> They revealed Dick, sitting far back in his corner, his coat collar
> turned up, his hands thrust in his pockets, and his broad dark
> hat shading him as if it were a part of him – a sort of wing he
> hid under. They showed her, sitting up very straight, her lovely
> little face more like a drawing than a real face – every line was so
> full of meaning and so sharp-cut against the swimming dark.
>
> (79–80)

Duquette is excited by what he sees as the performance in front of
him because he does not know what will happen next; he also
wants to be part of the action, and has to curb a powerful impetus
to behave 'like a clown. To start singing, with large extravagant gestures' (80). There is a sense that the whole episode between Harmon
and the woman is pre-scripted, but that Duquette has not encountered this particular narrative model before so he finds it piquant.
From the beginning of the story, he reiterates his sense that human
life is a series of narrative stereotypes, *plus ça change, plus c'est la
même chose*. He sees people as suitcases which have been packed
with different combinations of items; he is a Customs official who
has to decide whether to believe them when they state what they
have to declare. The motif of categorizing is emphasized as he con-
templates the 'moment of hesitation as to whether I am going to be
fooled just before I chalk that squiggle' (61); there seems to be no
doubt that people can be classified, though he may get the classification wrong. He draws the reader's attention to the banality of his
own paradigms; having described a winter scene he comments that
the Virgin Mary might have ridden into it on an ass:

> That's rather nice, don't you think, that bit about the Virgin? It
> comes from the pen so gently; it has such a 'dying fall.' I thought
> so at the time and decided to make a note of it. One never knows
> when a little tag like that may come in useful to round off a
> paragraph.
>
> (63)

The quotation from *Twelfth Night* is presented as a writerly creden-
tial, while the complacency of tone distances the reader from the
narrator and destabilizes the text. Whenever Duquette is left to
imagine a scene, he imagines something from formulaic melodrama.

When he asks the woman, in Harmon's absence, whether he can help, parentheses tell the reader the response he envisages: '(Soft music...)' (85). When she goes to look for Harmon, the narrator confides in the reader: 'You know I had the mad idea that they were kissing in that quiet room – a long, comfortable kiss' (86). His alternative is a violent one, and he sees it as a series of sensational newspaper photographs:

> Flash! went my mind. Dick has shot himself, and then a succession of flashes while I rushed in, saw the body, head unharmed, small blue hole over temple, roused hotel, arranged funeral, attended funeral, closed cab, new morning coat...
>
> (87)

As Perry Meisel observes: 'Such a perspective deracinates all notions of authenticity... Authenticity of self – or of world – is no more than a fiction, no less real for being so but surely less secure metaphysically.'[57]

The story can be read in the light of Bergson's distinction between a series of differentiated homogeneous moments and a heterogeneous dynamic. The narrator offers the reader a sequence of events, each sharply delineated by self-conscious metaphorical language, but the story also has a rhythmical counter-discourse of which the narrator seems unaware as he poses for the reader. It could be called Fauvist, in that it hints at a voracious wildness that is at odds with drinking tea in a crisis, and playing prescribed roles. Duquette's sentimental cynicism is evident from the titles of his books, *False Coins*, *Wrong Doors* and *Left Umbrellas*; his mind runs in well-oiled grooves. Just before he meets the woman, his preconceptions about English femininity convince him that 'she would be very severe, flat back and front, or she would be tall, fair, dressed in mignonette green, name – Daisy, and smelling of rather sweetish lavender water' (74–5). Every time his script is disrupted by the unexpected, he mentally rewrites it in an attempt to accommodate and subdue unpredictability. What the reader perceives is a Fauvist savagery in the story of which the narrator seems unconscious.

His sketch of the café at the beginning is heightened and exaggerated, expressionist in its impetus. Its palette is Fauvist: the waiter 'poured me out a glass of the familiar, purplish stuff with a green wandering light playing over it' (63). The clients at the counter are workmen, 'all powdered over with white flour, lime or something' (61), anticipating the narrator's longing to play a clown later in the story. The proprietor is equally spectral:

> Madame is thin and dark, too, with white cheeks and white hands. In certain lights she looks quite transparent, shining out of her black shawl with an extraordinary effect. When she is not serving she sits on a stool with her face turned, always, to the window. Her dark-ringed eyes search among and follow after the people passing... And then there is the waiter... He is grey, flat-footed and withered, with long, brittle nails that set your nerves on edge while he scrapes up your two sous. When he is not smearing over the table or flicking at a dead fly or two, he stands with one hand on the back of a chair.
>
> (61–2)

Evidently this is not a fleeting, impressionistic moment; there is a terrible permanence about it which is revealing about the state of mind of the narrator: what he notices is despair, obsession and decay. The waiter sounds cadaverous and Madame might be a vampire in search of sustenance, an undercurrent or rhythm that runs through the story. The only memory of his childhood that the narrator retains is of his family's African laundress who sucked his childhood away by beckoning him 'in a strange secret way' to a little outhouse where she kissed him, especially inside his ears: 'from that very first afternoon, my childhood was, to put it prettily, "kissed away." I became very languid, very caressing, and greedy beyond measure' (66). In the original version, which was cut in accordance with Michael Sadler's wishes when it was published by Constable, but appeared in full in the pamphlet printed by Murry and his brother for their Heron Press, the laundress is more overtly Fauvist: 'And then with a soft growl she tore open her bodice and put me to her.'[58] The African is constructed as exotic, uninhibited and sexually challenging, comparable with the Tahitian women in Gauguin's paintings; the narrator's experience with her is casually linked to the undead, when he comments: 'And enough of my childhood, too. Bury it under a laundry basket instead of a shower of roses and *passons outre*' (67).

The implication is that the blood of the tiny pale child has been sucked, and at some level he recognizes vampires when he encounters them. At the beginning of his acquaintance with the Englishman, Harmon drops a photograph of a woman: 'Not quite young. Dark, handsome, wild-looking, but so full in every line of a kind of haggard pride that even if Dick had not stretched out so quickly I wouldn't have looked longer' (72). The effect of the image is so strong that 'if he had not been Dick I should have been tempted to cross myself' (73); there is a strong suggestion that this woman preys on the vital juices of others. Just as the African laundress infected Duquette, Harmon's mother seems to have infected him. When he returns to Paris in the company of the young woman, as in vampire stories, he is almost unrecognizable, and he elicits an involuntary invocation, like the impulse to cross himself, from Duquette:

'Good God!' My smile and my lifted hand fell together. For one terrible moment I thought this was the woman of the photograph, Dick's mother, walking towards me in Dick's coat and hat. In the effort – and you saw what an effort it was – to smile, his lips curled in just the same way and he made for me, haggard and wild and proud.

(77)

The narrator makes no connections, but the reader can observe sinister recurrent images. Just as Harmon seems to have two selves, the narrator himself does. He sees himself in the mirror of the café and thinks: 'There I had been for all eternity, as it were, and now at last I was coming to life' (63). A repressed self haunts the pages of the story: 'All the while I wrote that last page my other self has been chasing up and down out in the dark there' (65). This is totally at odds with the banal phrases and stereotyped narratives he draws the reader's attention to, as is the woman's response to her lover's abandonment of her. Duquette suggests the predictable narrative line, that she will follow him back to England, but she is outraged and rejects the suggestion. Duquette does not understand why he never went near her again, not even to satisfy his curiosity: '*Je ne parle pas français*. That was her swan song for me' (90). What unnerves him, the reader may infer, is that she does not, literally or psychologically, speak his language; she lives without pigeon-holing, categorizing and stereotyping. His chic cynicism deserts him as he realizes: 'Why, they were suffering...those two...really suffering. I have seen two people suffer as I don't suppose I ever shall again...' (90).

Throughout the story, the unnamed woman, who wears grey fur, is called Mouse, by her lover and by the narrator, and Duquette defines himself as a fox-terrier. When Harmon departs for England unexpectedly, the narrator complains to himself: '"But after all it was you who whistled to me, you who asked me to come! What a spectacle I've cut wagging my tail and leaping round you"' (73–4). They are neat homogeneous images, but the deep structure of the story undermines their sentimental crispness. Duquette is not a fawning dog who assists his master with the hunt, he is himself in control of the prey. As a brutal predator, he uses both lecherous old men, whom he describes as dogs, and vulnerable girls: 'And so on and so on until some dirty old gallant comes up to my table and sits opposite and begins to grimace and yap. Until I hear myself saying: "But I've got the little girl for you, *mon vieux*. So little...so tiny"' (91). The final words of the story are chilling; they are an exchange between the narrator and the vampiric Madame, who seems in her customer to recognize her own kind, those who feed on the innocent:

> I must go. I must go. I reach down my coat and hat. Madame knows me. 'You haven't dined yet?' she smiles.
> 'No, not yet, Madame.'
>
> (91)

Mansfield's literary career pivoted on the deep structures explored in '*Je ne parle pas français*'. The exclusion both she and Fergusson experienced because they did not speak the language of Oxbridge and Bloomsbury led them to a colourist, Fauvist language, where line and structure could liberate them into a new means of expression. Her response to the liberating power of Post-Impressionism for her as a writer is expressed in a letter to the painter Brett, written when she was very ill in 1921 but remembering the impact on her of the exhibition that opened in the Grafton Galleries (not the Goupil) on 5 November 1910, 'Manet and the Post-Impressionists'. The specific paintings she is recalling are Van Gogh's *Sunflowers* and probably *The Postman Roulin*; she experienced the exhibition a year before she met Murry and Fergusson, but her reaction shows how receptive she would be to their excitement about expressionist initiatives in the arts:

> Wasn't that Van Gogh shown at the Goupil ten years ago? Yellow flowers – brimming with sun in a pot? I wonder if it is the same. That picture seemed to reveal something that I hadn't realised before I saw it. It lived with me afterwards. It still does – that & another of a sea captain in a flat cap. They taught me something about writing, which was queer – a kind of freedom – or rather, a shaking free. When one has been working for a long stretch one begins to narrow ones vision a bit, to fine things down too much. And its only when something else breaks through, a picture, or something seen out of doors that one realises it. It is – literally – years since I have been to a picture show. I can *smell* them as I write.[59]

2
The Little Colonial: 1888–1908

'I, a woman, with the taint of the pioneer in my blood'.[1]

In a political elegy, 'To Stanislaw Wyspianski', which Mansfield wrote celebrating the achievement of the Polish writer and patriot, she compares her country unfavourably with his. She seems to reproduce the banal analogy of Britain as the parent country and the colony as child, defining itself in relation to Europe; she comes from 'the other side of the world', appearing to accept that 'this' side is ancient, historical and significant:

> From a little land with no history,
> (Making its own history, slowly and clumsily
> Piecing together this and that, finding the pattern, solving the
>   problem,
> Like a child with a box of bricks)[2]

When she writes of herself as having 'the taint' of the pioneer in her blood, she apparently accepts her social inferiority to civilized Europeans, and the fact that to them she can never fully be a 'lidy'. New Zealanders are portrayed in the poem as crudely materialistic: 'What would they know of ghosts and unseen presences?' Yet one of the most significant aspects of Mansfield's early writing is her consciousness that being of pioneering stock may carry a taint that does not refer simply to social status in relation to the imperial power, but to land appropriation and attempted genocide.

This taboo subject is explored in one of her first publications, 'In the Botanical Gardens', a vignette that appeared in 1907 in the *Native*

Companion, a new monthly magazine published in Melbourne. In Australian writing of that period Aboriginal people are rarely mentioned except as trackers, servants and a menace to pioneer progress; finding a sympathetic engagement with Maori dispossession in a magazine that favoured stories about sex must have surprised its readers. Possibly that is why it appears under the pseudonym Julian Mark, whereas the other pieces by her that were published at the same time were attributed to K. Mansfield. The form that Mansfield devised for what she called vignettes enabled her to avoid the conclusiveness of a conventional narrative line; she told E. J. Brady, the editor of the *Native Companion*, that the vignettes 'feel very much my own – This style of work absorbs me, at present'.[3] Vincent O'Sullivan seems to see the vignettes themselves as a kind of pioneering in prose writing:

> They first proposed to her a freedom that already moved towards the stories she would later write, easing emotion away from the need to account for it fully, allowing an adjectival assault on the notion that one needed to be either consistent or explanatory. They were excursions into that dimly defined territory between the expectations of prose and the freer emotional contours of verse.[4]

Her other vignettes in the *Native Companion* are solipsistic mood pieces in a style that reveals her fascination with Wilde: 'the grey thoughts fall upon my soul like the grey rain upon the world'.[5] 'In the Botanical Gardens', however, engages obliquely with the nature of colonialism, its repressions and its guilt; the subject itself suggests veneration of that Mecca of colonial travel, the Royal Botanic Gardens at Kew.

As early as this – Mansfield was 19 – she identifies Impressionism with surface realism: within 'the orthodox banality of carpet bedding' in the Central Walk of the Botanical Gardens, people 'seem as meaningless, as lacking in individuality, as the little figures in an impressionist landscape'.[6] Unexpectedly, the Decadents are not entirely absent from the evocation of the scene in the gardens; anemones 'always appear to me a trifle dangerous, sinister, seductive but poisonous'.[7] This seduction is one of the alternatives offered by the 'artificial' part of the gardens; it is all contained within the

Enclosure, within the boundaries that form a crucial part of colonial life, and are reproduced within the gardens. When the speaker turns from 'the smooth swept paths' to a steep track, she becomes dimly aware of another history and a different way of living with the land; 'the bush' in New Zealand means the forest or the wild:

> And, suddenly, it disappears, all the pretty, carefully-tended surface of gravel and sward and blossom, and there is bush, silent and splendid. On the green moss, on the brown earth, a wide splashing of yellow sunlight. And, everywhere that strange, indefinable scent. As I breathe it, it seems to absorb, to become part of me – and I am old with the age of centuries, strong with the strength of savagery.

The manicured landscape gives way to something that smells different: the 'yellow scent' of cowslips and the 'chiming' of daffodils, that icon of English nature that colonial children had to encounter through Wordsworth's poem, are displaced by a smell that transforms the speaker. The impetus of the passage is the speaker's need to identify with this bifurcating experience.

The language is sometimes facile and glib, depending on stereotypes of savagery and antiquity, and offering the thin explanation of 'magic' for the speaker's contradictory sense of self, but there is also a political and radical vision at work in the passage. She puts her hands into the water of a little stream:

> An inexplicable persistent feeling seizes me that I must become one with it all. Remembrance has gone – this is the Lotus Land – the green trees stir languorously ... Oh is it magic? Shall I, looking intently, see vague forms lurking in the shadow staring at me malevolently, wildly, the thief of their birthright? Shall I, down the hillside, through the bush, ever in the shadow, see a great company moving towards me, their faces averted, wreathed with green garlands, passing, passing, following the little stream in silence until it is sucked into the wide sea ... [8]

The cultural frame of reference is western: stealing the birthright derives from the story of Esau and Jacob, and gestures towards a betrayal of brotherhood.[9] The Lotus Land comes from Tennyson's

'The Lotos-Eaters', itself a poem about the colonial process, and the sailors' temptation to forget links with the 'Fatherland' to become part of a drugged and sensuous present. The speaker wants to identify with disruption and division. If she 'becomes one' with the great company with averted faces, she is aligning herself with death. The phrase 'passing, passing' from the shore to the wide sea suggests annihilation, hinting at social Darwinism, the contemporary white belief that 'inferior' races would eventually become extinct. Comparing the sound of the trees to weeping, the speaker moves to the entrance gates, and juxtaposes the two elements of her cultural being:

> The men and women and children are crowding the pathway, looking reverently, admiringly, at the carpet bedding, spelling aloud the Latin names of the flowers.
> Here is laughter and movement and bright sunshine – but, behind me … is it near, or miles and miles away … the bush lies, hidden in the shadow.[10]

The reverence shown by the crowd is for European civilization: Latin names derive from Linnaean plant classification, and carpet bedding suggests imitation of seafront parades and municipal flower beds at respectable resorts on the south coast of England. The repressed aspect of the self, which she has tried to bring into the open by smelling and touching the wild landscape, remains a shadow, 'behind me', possibly close but out of reach. However 'the bush' is not constructed as everything that is inimical to the pioneer, as it is in most writing of the period, and it is not empty, but is filled with a great spectral company of reproachful and betrayed people. The content as well as the form of this vignette show an originality and complexity of vision in its young writer.

This chapter focuses on Mansfield's childhood and young womanhood in New Zealand, and her education there and in Britain, concentrating on her developing awareness of divisions in the self. She was torn between a European Decadent aesthetic and political hostility to the ways in which the British class system had been replicated in New Zealand; between love of her family and resentment of their bourgeois expectations; between wanting to be as popular as her sisters and wanting to trangress sexual and racial boundaries; between London and New Zealand.

Mansfield's father's family were of pioneering stock. Her father, Harold Beauchamp, was born in the Australian gold fields, amid the diggings at Ararat; his father was a colonial drifter, whose example Harold was anxious not to follow. Harold worked for, and then became a partner in and eventually owner of Bannatyne's, an importing firm; he moved inexorably up the social scale in the colonial capital, Wellington, which called itself 'The Empire City', with his many changes of address signalling his upwardly mobile status. Eventually he had a knighthood and was a director of companies, as well as being elected chairman of the board of the Bank of New Zealand. He had a cousin, Fred, who had a Maori wife and five sons, but Harold repressed this knowledge and omitted it from his autobiography, *Reminiscences and Recollections*. Mansfield's mother, Annie Dyer, was born in Sydney to the wife of an insurance clerk for the Australian Mutual Provident Society; he was sent to Wellington to open the first New Zealand branch, and died there in debt in 1877. Harold Beauchamp had fallen in love with Annie Dyer when she was 14. They married in 1884, when she was 20, and had six children in ten years: Kathleen Mansfield Beauchamp was the third; the fourth died in infancy; the last, Leslie, was the only boy. 'Mansfield' was the maiden name of Kathleen's dearly loved maternal grandmother, a love reflected in what became the writer's pseudonym, Katherine Mansfield. Mansfield's parents were devoted to each other and created a strong sense of the family as a unit; Annie's widowed mother and her two unmarried sisters lived with them when they were first married. The Beauchamp children were well educated for their period; though there was an emphasis on respectability and gentility, music, painting, debate and social awareness were part of the intellectual context that their father offered them:

> Annie Burnell Beauchamp dressed her children well, and passed on to them the little snobberies, those glancing condescensions, that Kathleen would never lose. Mainly because of her father, one supposes, the large, fashionable house in Fitzherbert Terrace was open to Catholic priests, to Jewish business friends, to visiting artistes. Harold even made a point of speaking Maori. For its day, and its place, the family was spared the grosser prejudices of its community. For all Kathleen's complaining, her parents were tolerant, the girls supervised rather than ruled.[11]

Mansfield's first school was in the country township of Karori where she and her family lived in a house called 'Chesney Wold'; the use of the name as a cultural signifier might have amused her later, as it is the home of the rigid Sir Leicester Dedlock in Dickens's *Bleak House*. Sir Leicester is so hidebound by his devotion to the British class structure that he fails to communicate his deep feelings for his wife, resulting indirectly in her death and his paralysis. There is evidence of Mansfield's resistance to injustice from her time at Karori school: 'When the teacher of the school rebuked a lad for sleeping at his desk, Kathleen spoke up to explain that he was forced to rise at three o'clock each morning to help with the family milk delivery, and the boy escaped a caning.'[12] She was moved to Wellington Girls' High School, a less egalitarian environment, when she was nine; when she was ten she moved again, this time to Miss Swainson's private school, where there were several Jewish pupils and a Maori girl, Maata Mahupuku. Early in 1903 she sailed for London with her sisters, and became a pupil at Queen's College, Harley Street. There were family reasons for choosing the school, but it also confirms O'Sullivan's observations about the Beauchamp parents' positive qualities, in that it

> had been founded in 1848 with the aim of cultivating individual-
> ity and free intellectual endeavour in its pupils rather than cram-
> ming them with facts or moulding them into pre-ordained
> shapes...Discipline was not strict: there was no uniform, and
> girls were allowed out in pairs to explore London.[13]

Her own background in New Zealand and her freedom in London encouraged her interest in painting; throughout her letters and notebooks this preoccupation is evident. When she was at Queen's College she wrote a poem beginning 'This is my world'; it lists her treasures and includes 'my pictures that line the wall. / Yes, that is a Doré'.[14] In her first vignette she paints a colourist picture of the hills round Wellington and characterizes it in painterly terms:

> A white road round the hills – there I walked – And below me –
> like a beautiful Pre Raphaelite picture – lay the sea – and the vio-
> let mountains. The sky all a riot of rose and yellow – amethyst
> and purple.[15]

The painters that she mentions in early letters and notebooks have a more romantic vision than the Post-Impressionists she responds to with such a sense of liberation in December 1910. After leaving school, back in New Zealand and yearning for London, she writes in 1907 to her cousin, who had also been a pupil at Queen's College: 'There is nothing on earth to do – nothing to see – and my heart keeps flying off – Oxford Circus – Westminster Bridge at the Whistler hour.'[16] She seems to be thinking of one of Whistler's twilight riverscapes, and to be missing the mystery and menace of the foggy city streets that were explored in the work of her favourite writers as well as painters: Wilde gestures towards Whistler's *Nocturne in Blue and Gold: Old Battersea Bridge* in his poem '*Impression du Matin*':

> The Thames nocturne of blue and gold
>   Changed to a harmony in grey;
>   A barge with ochre-coloured hay
> Dropped from the wharf: and chill and cold
>
> The yellow fog came creeping down
>   The bridges, till the houses' walls
>   Seemed changed to shadows, and St Paul's
> Loomed like a bubble o'er the town.

In a bracingly school-mistressy letter to her sister, Mansfield scolds her fellow-countrymen for failing to respond to this kind of poetry; they must pull themselves together and cleanse themselves of materialism by taking a good dose of purifying decadence. It is an odd prescription in that it seems to lack irony, but it shows the young writer's confidence in her own intellectual judgement:

> I am ashamed of young New Zealand, but what is to be done. All the firm fat framework of their brains must be demolished before they can begin to learn. They want a purifying influence – a mad wave of pre-Raphaelitism, of super-aestheticism, should intoxicate the country. They must go to excess in the direction of culture, become almost decadent in their tendencies for a year or two and then find balance and proportion. We want two or three persons gathered together to discuss line and form and atmosphere and sit at the street corners, in the shops, in the houses, at the Teas.[17]

A Tea seems a curious arena for an evangelist of decadence to make converts, but it is significant that Mansfield's concern with attempting to reconcile her two worlds, and her preoccupation with line and form, are evident when she is only 19. In a more incisive entry in a notebook which shows how thoroughly she has absorbed Wilde's aphorisms, she writes: 'When N[ew] Z[ealand] is more artificial she will give birth to an artist who can treat her natural beauties adequately. This sounds paradoxical but is true.'[18] She recognizes from the beginning of her career that all representation is artifice, and that realism is no more natural than any other artistic mode. Any art requires its practitioner to study techniques of artifice. In the little lists of tasks that punctuate the notebooks, a revealing one for 1907 reads:

Timetable
6–8   technique
9–1   practise
2–5   write
            Freedom[19]

This may mean that the evening brings freedom, but alternatively that mastering an art is liberating.

Mansfield's home life and her schooling gave her access to libraries and plenty of time to read. A list taken at random from the notebooks for 1908 reads:

Does Oscar – and there is a gardenia yet alive beside my bed – does Oscar still keep so firm a stronghold in my soul? No! Because now I am growing capable of seeing a wider vision – a little Oscar, a little Symons, a little Dolf Wyllarde, Ibsen, Tolstoi, Elizabeth Robins, Shaw, D'Annunzio, Meredith.[20]

Wilde is the dominant literary presence in the early notebooks, with pages of quotation from him defining the life of an aesthete. His influence on her writing is evident in the early vignettes. 'Study: The Death of a Rose' has a prurient and necrophiliac tone; yesterday the rose had a 'certain serene, tearful, virginal beauty' but

Today it is heavy and languid with the loves of a thousand strange Things, who, lured by the gold of my candlelight, came in the Purple Hours, and kissed it hotly on the mouth, and sucked it into their beautiful lips with tearing, passionate desire.[21]

Wilde might have wanted to edit this, especially the cautious and uninspired use of 'Things', but the passage shows that experiment with symbolism and colour, with tone, and with the rhythm of prose sentences is part of Mansfield's rigorous training of herself as a writer.

Mansfield's letters to her sister Vera convey a sense that books were discussed and exchanged at home, in spite of her complaints that when she is alone her family 'come outside the door and call to each other – discuss the butchers orders or the soiled linen, and, I feel, wreck my life'.[22] There is some affectation in her letters to Vera, but also a lively exchange of gossip and ideas that indicates what reading means to her. She feels that her intensity about it alienates her from the colonial world of which she is a part. Writing of Swinburne and William Morris she asks:

> Isn't it extraordinary how one can never tire of these people – they are my very good friends – and I know them immeasurably better than the people I meet here – There is a fascination almost unequalled in collecting all the detail's of a man's life – studying his portrait – his work – bringing him, splendidly willing, to one's own fireside – I have R. L. S. and Dante Gabriel Richard Wagner & Jimmy Whistler – *all* the Brontës – haven't you? One day let us give a dream party.[23]

What unites the writers she lists is their focus on the passions; she shows how she has internalized Catherine's account of her love for Heathcliff in *Wuthering Heights* when she writes to her lover, Garnet Trowell: 'If *all* the world left me and you remained then Life would be full – if *all* the world came to me and you were not here, in my soul, then Life would be empty.'[24]

Apart from Wilde, the writers who most evidently affected her literary development were Walter Pater and Arthur Symons. In 1908 she speculates on the possibility of writing a life in the style of Pater's 'The Child in the House': 'I'd make her a half caste Maori & call her Maata'.[25] The girl would leave Wellington and go to Europe 'to live there a dual existence'[26] as Mansfield felt she herself did.

Though she did plan and partially write a novel that she called *Maata*, it was not in the style of Pater's story; however, the portrayal of the consciousness of the child, Florian, in Pater's piece evidently interested Mansfield. Florian is an aesthetic Maggie Tulliver, valuing familiar things for their beauty, though the adult interpretative voice resembles that of the narrator of *The Mill on the Floss* and is unlike the mobile narrator of 'Prelude':

> Our susceptibilities…belong to this or the other well-remembered place in the material habitation – that little white room with the window across which the heavy blossoms could beat so peevishly in the wind, with just that particular catch or throb, such a sense of teasing in it, on gusty mornings; and the early habitation thus gradually becomes a sort of material shrine or sanctuary of sentiment; a system of visible symbolism interweaves itself through all our thoughts and passions.[27]

Mansfield's mature work, such as 'Prelude', would never articulate this as Pater does here; nevertheless, 'Prelude' shows without comment from the narrator a pattern of symbolism weaving itself from Linda's to Kezia's consciousness, most obviously in the aloe. Florian's experience of nostalgia and homesickness is analysed rather than imaged as Kezia's is in the second part of 'Prelude', but the intensity of a small child's awareness of memory and sense of desolation is conveyed with comparable vividness. Florian returns to a house that he and his family have just vacated, to rescue a pet bird that has been forgotten:

> But as he passed in search of it from room to room, lying so pale, with a look of meekness in their denudation, and at last through that little, stripped white room, the aspect of the place touched him like the face of one dead; and a clinging back towards it came over him, so intense that he knew it would last long.[28]

Pater does not convey in his own narrative that mobile, elusive, glimmering sense of the world that he theorizes so powerfully in his 'Conclusion' to *The Renaissance*, but Mansfield does. This was a pivotal text for her; she tried to live by Pater's dictum: 'To burn always with this hard, gemlike flame, to maintain this ecstasy, is success in life.'[29] His analysis of the nature of the self, shifting and impermanent, not a monolithic identity as it is, for instance, in *Middlemarch*, influenced her thinking as it did Virginia Woolf's, preparing her to recognize the significance that the *Rhythm* group assigned to intuition. Pater writes:

> To such a tremulous wisp constantly re-forming itself on the stream, to a single sharp impression, with a sense in it, a relic more or less fleeting, of such moments gone by, what is real in our life fines itself down. It is with this movement, with the passage and dissolution of impressions, images, sensations, that analysis leaves off – that continual vanishing away, that strange, perpetual weaving and unweaving of ourselves.[30]

Mansfield's awareness of the possibilities of symbolism was developed through her reading of Arthur Symons; his influence is evident in an essay that she and Murry wrote for *Rhythm*, 'Seriousness in Art', where they claim: 'Art is a perpetual striving towards an ever more adequate symbolic expression of the living realities of the world.'[31] Symons believes that the old bonds of description and rhetoric have to be broken if literature is to fulfil its destiny:

> Here, then, in this revolt against exteriority, against rhetoric, against a materialistic tradition; in this endeavour to disengage the ultimate essence, the soul, of whatever exists and can be realised by the consciousness; in this dutiful waiting upon every symbol by which the soul of things can be made visible; literature, bowed down by so many burdens, may at last attain liberty, and its authentic speech.[32]

The influence of Symons on Mansfield's speculations about art is evident throughout her notebooks: 'In as much as art seems to me *pure vision* I am indeed a partisan of objectivity', not of analysis.[33] This does not refer to impartiality, but to dwelling on the physical presence of things.

The other father figure who pervades Mansfield's writing usually provokes an outburst of resistance: 'I cannot – will not – build a house upon any damned rock.'[34] The Bible and the *Book of Common Prayer*, like Shakespeare, are echoed in the cadences of Mansfield's prose throughout her life, as well as being consciously quoted. The tension between her alternative fathers is expressed in an early draft for a novel, 'Juliet'. The protagonist is, like Mansfield, torn between London and New Zealand:

> On the one hand lay the mode bohème – alluring, knowledge-bringing, full of work and sensation, full of impulse, pulsating with the cry of Youth Youth Youth ... On the other hand lay the Suitable Appropriate Existence. The days full of perpetual Society functions, the hours full of clothes discussions – the waste of life. The stifling atmosphere would kill me, she thought.[35]

This fairly simple alternative is constantly complicated in the early writing by her awareness of the *taint* of the pioneer, the repressed history of the dispossession of the Maoris. When she was 13 she wrote exuberantly on the flyleaf of her prayerbook, after she had heard the Rev. Fred Bennett give a sermon on 'Mauries': 'The most heavenly thing possible. He also read the Second lesson. The Betrayal of Jesus. I never enjoyed myself so much. I am going to be a Mauri missionary.'[36] There is one piece of evidence that she corresponded with Mother Mary Joseph Aubert, a French nun who worked as a missioner with the Maoris and might have been somewhat sceptical about Mansfield's relish for the betrayal of Jesus, but no more is recorded of this crusading ambition. The notebooks are punctuated from the beginning with Maori phrases, translations and stories; one notebook contains a diary record of Mansfield's camping trip in 1907 to Urewera, edited by Ian Gordon and published as a separate text, *The Urewera Notebook*, in 1979. This contains vivid and mostly unedited notes on what she saw:

> We camped on the top of a hill, mountains all round & in the evening walked in the bush – to a beautiful daisy pied creek – ferns, tuis, & we saw the sheep sheds – smell & sound – 12 Maoris – their hoarse crying, dinner cooking in the homestead, the roses, the Maori cook.[37]

She tries to learn Maori, and lists phrases with their translations; her sense that she cannot communicate extends to the landscape: 'it is all so gigantic and tragic & even in the bright sunlight it is so passionately secret.'[38] She seems to be reading into the landscape what she may know but does not overtly mention about the Maori Wars; when they travel at night she writes:

> Visions of long dead Maoris, of forgotten battles and vanished feuds stirred in me – till I ran through the dark glade on to a bare hill – the track was very narrow & steep. And at the summit a little Maori whare was painted black against the wide sky.[39]

'Feuds' suggests conflict between different Maori peoples, so she is possibly distancing herself from her people's part in New Zealand history, but she observes the frailty of the Maori children and is conscious of absence:

> [We] pass several little whares, deserted & grey. They look very old and desolate – almost haunted – on the door there is a horse collar or a torn or scribbled notice – flowers in the garden, one clump of golden broom, one clump of yellow irises.[40]

When she describes children, they are not constructed as mysteriously other: 'The small boy is raggedly dressed in brown, his clothes are torn in many places, he wears a brown felt hat with a "koe-koea" feather placed rakishly to the side.'[41] Her encounters with adults produce more stereotypical accounts of the native as sexually potent, but mentally sluggish with a primeval torpor. In a vignette she creates a young Maori girl: 'All the lines of her face are passionate, violent, crudely savage, but in her lifted eyes slumbers a tragic illimitable Peace.'[42] Mansfield's mood-swings during the Urewera trip are violent, from 'We laugh with joy all day'[43] to 'Feel fearfully low',[44] as if her intense involvement with the place produces extreme reactions: 'Give me the Maori and the tourist but nothing between.'[45]

Contact with Maori families was a revelation which intrigued her; talking to a 'worn but rather beautiful' mother of five children she was told: 'It is in Winter that it is so cold, all snow & they sit by the fire, never go out at all, just sit with many clothes on & smoke.'[46] First-hand experience of Maori life may account for her emotive reaction to the trip; they had been part of her imaginative life long before this encounter with reality. The theme of 'Summer Idylle', the piece that appears in her notebook for 1906, is a curious merging of myths, with homoerotic implications. From the beginning, the language is sensuous, with an emphasis on physical stimulus. The animism of the passage creates the sea as a lover, arousing desire in the girl:

> A slow tranquil surrender of the Night Spirits, a knowledge that her body was refreshed and cool and light, a great breath from the sea that skimmed through the window & kissed her laughingly – and her awakening was complete.[47]

The sea is surprisingly gendered as female when the protagonist, Hinemoa, slips out of bed to gaze at it, anticipating the sexual relationship that unfolds:

> The sea shone with such an intense splendour – danced, leapt up, cried aloud, ran along the line of white beach so daintily, drew back so shyly, & then flung itself on to the warm whiteness with so complete an abandon.
>
> (75)

There is a rather prurient sense of childish sexuality here, which sets the tone for the story. Hinemoa in Maori legend had to swim to an island to join her lover, but in Mansfield's story Hinemoa is pakeha, and Marina, her friend whose name links her with European legend and Shakespeare's *Pericles*, is a Maori. Hinemoa leaves her own bedroom and enters Marina's, which is heady with the sensuousness of manuka blossom. She bends over her friend's bed, dazed with pleasure and, by implication, desire: 'It came upon her if she had used too much perfume, if she had drunk wine that was too heavy & sweet, laid her hand on velvet that was too soft & smooth' (75). Marina is 'wrapped in the darkness of her hair' whereas she calls Hinemoa 'Snow Maiden – Snow Maiden', accentuating both their skin colour and Hinemoa's willed innocence in comparison with her friend: Hinemoa feels a sensation of pleasure 'which she did not analyse'. When Marina throws manuka blossoms at Hinemoa, who cries 'O come quick, come quick' and Marina replies 'I come now', the orgasmic intensity becomes overt.

They swim to an island, where Marina instructs Hinemoa in reading the landscape. Hinemoa refers to the arms of fern trees, but Marina corrects her, saying that fern trees have beautiful green hair, not arms; they are gendered as female, and wrap warriors in their hair in order to kill them, linking the ferns with Marina as the reader first sees her, wrapped in her dark hair. Stereotypes of savagery, anticipating Mansfield's engagement with Fauvism, blend with sado-masochism as Marina tells Hinemoa she would like to be cruel to her, and she looks at her 'with half-shut eyes, her upper lip drawn back showing her teeth' (76). Both girls dive from a rock keeping their eyes open, the Maori instructing the pakeha, who feels a 'flood of excitement'. Curiously Hinemoa then swims back to the shore and runs in to kiss her own image in the mirror: 'What a fright you had, dear' (76). The dive seems to be a kind of birthing into both sexuality and Maori life, which she then rejects by panicking and confirming her whiteness by kissing it, using a banal quasi-maternal phrase to re-establish her white identity. Sydney Janet Kaplan interprets this episode through a comparison with a much later story by D. H. Lawrence, 'The Horse-Dealer's Daughter':

> But as in Lawrence's story, the return to the ordinary after the plunge contains elements of retrogression. The dive is so over-powering, so destructive of the known and the assured, that although everything is changed forever it seems necessary to seek, at least momentarily, comfort from the familiar. And comfort as well from the protection of the shell of the ego.[48]

Hinemoa's sexual arousal is suggested again when she eats a peach with the juice running through her fingers, but she is too reticent to meet Marina's challenge. Marina has cooked kumaras, sweet potatoes, which turn blue when they are cooked, but Hinemoa will not eat them because 'they're too unnatural'. Marina, on the other hand, says: 'I eat it for that reason … I eat it because it is blue' (77). The desire for the other is expressed potently, its transgression emphasized by crossing racial and homoerotic boundaries in a story that has the ingredients of an apparently innocent fairy tale. Marina's power stems from her freedom from conventional norms: she does not need a mirror to give her a sense of identity, and is unconstrained by dictates about social behaviour. Hinemoa's experience combines rites of passage from different cultures; she dives with her eyes open, but then 'dressed slowly & gravely in a straight white gown' (76) as if she were ready for her first communion, which is also hinted at in the final phrase of the story, 'breaking the bread in her white fingers' (77). Part of what Mansfield seems to have recognized on the Urewera trip was that codes of behaviour and initiation exist in all cultures, though they may not resemble pakeha conventions.

Mansfield treasured a ring she was given by the Maoris, eventually giving it to her lover, William Orton. She seems to have told Ida Baker some mystifying nonsense about it which may have been part of one of her disguises; Baker comments: 'It had been given to her by the Maoris, and had some strange significance and occult power.'[49] The obsession with alternative selves, the Marina/Hinemoa doubling, is inextricably bound up with Mansfield's cultural preoccupations at this time in her life, possibly specifically with *The Picture of Dorian Gray*. She writes in her notebooks about various lesbian relationships. When she is involved with Edith Bendall she asks:

> O Oscar! Am I peculiarly susceptible to sexual impulse? I must be I suppose, but I rejoice. Now each time I see her I want her to put her arms round me & hold me against her. I think she wants to too, but she is afraid, & Custom hedges her in.[50]

At the same time she is frightened by what she sees as her own drive to destruction and issues warnings: 'PULL UP NOW YOURSELF.'[51] When she was eleven, at Miss Swainson's school, one of her closest friends was a Maori girl, Maata Mahupuku; their relationship later developed into a sexual one in which Mansfield pursued Mahupuku. Mahupuku fascinated some of Mansfield's early biographers because she was half Maori, and was known as a 'princess'. In his little book speculating about whether Mansfield had written a novel about her, published in 1946, Pat Lawlor reproduces the stereotypical constructions, characteristic of his period, of Maoris as both primitive and exotic. He met Mahupuku and writes that she has 'a Mona Lisa smile'[52] and is 'anything but the fat, round-faced, thick-lipped Maori woman with whom we are familiar in this country'[53] as if Maoris did not belong in New Zealand. He is guarded about what Mahupuku tells him of her relationship with Mansfield: 'Maata went on to refer to other rather sensational aspects of her alleged knowledge of Katherine Mansfield.'[54] Mansfield's notebooks are not similarly restrained. In some places her sexual longing for other women, including Mahupuku, is expressed without inhibition, though with anxiety about notional norms which she feels she crosses. She adds a cultural rider to sanction her behaviour:

> Do other people of my own age feel as I do I wonder so absolutely powerful <u>licentious</u>, so almost physically ill. I alone in this silent clock filled room have become powerfully – – – I want Maata. I want her as I have had her – terribly. This is unclean I know but true. What an extraordinary thing – I feel savagely crude, and almost powerfully enamoured of the child. I had thought that a thing of the Past. Heigh Ho!!!!!!!!!!! My mind is like a Russian novel.[55]

A different dimension to her preoccupation with women is a growing feminism; though she was not a suffragette she thought that 'this suffragist movement is *excellent* for our sex'.[56] She did go to Suffrage meetings but 'decided I could not be a suffragette – the world was too full of laughter'.[57] She came, through reading *Come and Find Me*, by an American actor, Elizabeth Robins, to 'feel that I do now realise, dimly, what women in the future will be capable of achieving...Talk of our enlightened days and our emancipated country – pure nonsense. We are firmly held in the self fashioned chains of slavery.'[58] The versions of Mansfield's life that focus on her relationship with her family are inclined to minimize the kind of political awareness that is evident in this passage; the astute observation that the chains are *self*-fashioned leads her into active awareness of the ways in which women restrict themselves by acquiescing in the dictates of patriarchy. Her mature stories interrogate those norms, often through comedy in a domestic situation, as for instance in 'Prelude', when Linda hangs cherries over the ear of the conquering hero who has just returned from the office.

The range of tones of voice quoted so far from the notebooks indicates the truth of Ida Baker's observation that she 'was a born actress and mimic'.[59] Using the ability to imitate, from her earliest stories she explores the 'self fashioned chains of slavery' of western and pakeha life, sometimes exposing their oddity by comparing them with other ways of being. This chapter concludes with a consideration of two stories, 'How Pearl Button was Kidnapped' and 'The Doll's House'. 'How Pearl Button was Kidnapped' was written in 1910 and published in *Rhythm* in 1912 under the pseudonym Lili

Heron; 'The Doll's House' was first published in the *Athenaeum* in 1922. In both stories the protagonist, a little girl, swings on the gate; both children are transgressive, in that they want either to get out of the world for which the gate is a demarcation line, or to admit outsiders to the well-regulated inside world. In the early story the alternatives are posed quite simply but surprisingly for the period. What makes it interesting is that the perspective is the child's, and she does not categorize as an adult would. The expectations raised by the title are not fulfilled; there is no tension in the story, the reader is not invited to hope that the child will be rescued, but it is not either a narrative of the 'Off with the wraggle-taggle gypsies' kind. The title gives an adult perspective on the events, but since the child enjoys the adventure, she does not perceive what happens as kidnapping.

Pearl Button thinks of her home as 'the House of Boxes'. The phrase is never explained, but the reader gains some clues as to what it means: when Pearl is asked where her mother is, she replies that she is in the kitchen 'ironing-because-its-Tuesday'.[60] She is frightened by the beach but there 'were some little houses down close to the sea, with wood fences round them and gardens inside. They comforted her' (522). A constraining boundary, with nature under control, is what she is familiar with. Eventually she asks the women who have 'kidnapped' her: 'Haven't you got any Houses of Boxes?…Don't you all live in a row? Don't the men go to offices? Aren't there any nasty things?' (522). When she is frightened she craves for the familiar order of bourgeois life, but increasingly she enjoys disorder: eating a peach and letting the juice run over her clothes and being kissed and cuddled by the two maternal women. The reader gradually realizes who the kidnappers are, but since race does not matter to Pearl she does not perceive it. The men wear 'feather mats round their shoulders' (521), one of the women is wearing a tiki, a greenstone amulet, and they live and travel in community groups; Pearl sees their difference but not that they are Maoris. The pivotal moment in the story comes when they reach the sea; Pearl is terrified of it but the Maoris coax her into it as Marina taught Hinemoa to dive in 'Summer Idylle'. At the moment that she begins to paddle she is released into a wider life, in which she can express herself spontaneously; the text's short sentences enact the infant consciousness, using objects, like a cup, which she is familiar with from the House of Boxes, modulating into a narratorial voice with the observation of the child's thin arms:

> She paddled in the shallow water. It was warm. She made a cup of her hands and caught some of it. But it stopped being blue in her hands. She was so excited that she rushed over to her woman and flung her little thin arms round the woman's neck, hugging her, kissing...
>
> (523)

At this point the transience of the natural world, which excites her with its novelty by changing colour as she looks at it, is replaced by much more substantial 'Little men in blue coats – little blue men' who have come 'to carry her back to the House of Boxes'. Her perception, and so the reader's, is that the prison-house is closing on her again, and that the uniformed men are jailers rather than liberators. This is how the Maori writer Witi Ihimaera interprets the story in his homage to it, 'The Affectionate Kidnappers'.[61]

   The doll's house in the second story has in some ways the same connotations as the House of Boxes. The children's excitement when the doll's house arrives seems depressingly incestuous. They appear, in gazing at the verisimilitude of the house, to be looking in at their own lives, especially when they see the 'father and mother dolls, who sprawled very stiff as though they had fainted in the drawing-room' (384). The reader has already been given a sense of the stiffness of the adults in the supercilious and falsely effusive tone of the opening paragraph: 'For, really, the smell of paint coming from that doll's house ("Sweet of old Mrs Hay, of course: most sweet and generous!") – but the smell of paint was quite enough to make anyone seriously ill' (383). Mansfield's mimicry is in evidence here; it is obvious where the many exaggerated stresses must fall. But one child perceives what the others do not notice, 'an exquisite little amber lamp' which 'seemed to smile at Kezia, to say, "I live here"' (384). This is the side of domestic life that counters the sprawling dolls; there is snobbery in the house but there is also light and warmth. In other stories about the Burnells the lamp is a signifier of understanding between women and girls: Kezia's grandmother in 'Prelude' asks her if she can '"trust you to carry the lamp?" "Yes, my granma." The old woman bent down and gave the bright breathing thing into her hands' (18).

The fact that Kezia's sisters have not noticed the lamp indicates their priorities. They identify with the sneer evident in Aunt Belle's attitude to old Mrs Hay, and their particular victims are the two little Kelvey girls:

> They were the daughters of a spry, hard-working little washerwoman, who went about from house to house by the day. This was awful enough. But where was Mr Kelvey? Nobody knew for certain. But everybody said he was in prison. So they were the daughters of a washerwoman and a gaolbird. Very nice company for other people's children!
>
> (386)

The mimicry is subtle here, beginning with a mildly sympathetic description of Mrs Kelvey, if Mrs she be, a possibility too shocking to contemplate, though it is an underlying question. The passage then shifts its narrative perspective to local gossip, showing how snobbish guesses quickly become accepted until the false logic culminates in the justification for ostracizing the little Kelveys; it is done with deft concision. The evocation of our Else is even more concise; she is 'a tiny wishbone of a child' (386), a visual description which also conveys Else's yearning. Her name suggests that she is doomed to be the other, the someone else, of polite society. After the little Kelveys have been publicly humiliated in the playground, the other children experience a quasi-sexual pleasure in it: 'the little girls rushed away in a body, deeply, deeply excited, wild with joy' (388–9). Their pleasure resembles Belle's, at the end of the story, when, having been intimidated by a lover, 'she had frightened those little rats of Kelveys and given Kezia a good scolding'. This releases her tension: 'That ghastly pressure was gone. She went back to the house humming' (390–1). The implication is that social and sexual scoring are closely aligned.

When the Burnell children return home from school after the playground episode, Kezia's two sisters, 'who liked visitors', enter the house but Kezia stays outside, on the gate, between the family and the Kelveys. Her potential for transgression is implied in the use of 'thieved':

> But Kezia thieved out at the back. Nobody was about; she began to swing on the big white gates of the courtyard … Kezia stopped

swinging. She slipped off the gate as if she was going to run away. Then she hesitated. The Kelveys came nearer, and beside them walked their shadows, very long, stretching right across the road with their heads in the buttercups. Kezia clambered back on the gate; she had made up her mind; she swung out.

(389)

Kezia is tempted to avoid the encounter but is prevented by the Kelveys' shadows, as if she recognizes in them the shadowy version of themselves that always accompanies the two little girls: the malicious gossip about their parents and background. When Kezia swings out she is opening both the doll's house and her own world to the two dispossessed children, though she remains in control, as her sisters did when their visitors came in groups of two to see the doll's house. Bourgeois life continues to be a spectacle to be admired and envied, but Else notices what Kezia likes best. When she and her sister have been routed by Belle, she rests beside her sister, stroking the quill on her sister's hat, and says 'I seen the little lamp' (391). The lamp, as in 'Prelude', seems to represent a perception and domestic warmth that women and girls can, but do not necessarily, share. The final isolated line of the story implies that the momentary rapport cannot affect social barriers for Lil and Else: 'Then both were silent once more' (391).

'How Pearl Button was Kidnapped' was written at the beginning of Mansfield's professional life; it is described by Sam Hynes as an escape fantasy[62] but Pearl's temporary escape from the House of Boxes leads the reader into a recognition of Maori entrapment. The narrative prioritizes Pearl's predicament as it uses her perspective, but the unanswered question about what happens to the Maori kidnappers remains. Neither is there any indication of why they take the child; the narrative method reveals the pakeha assumption that the settlers' interests are paramount, and it enacts the taint of the pioneer in its apparent indifference to the fate of the Maoris. 'The Doll's House' was one of the last stories Mansfield wrote; Gardner McFall speculates that it may have been written as a result of a correspondence Mansfield had about one of Brett's paintings:

> The portion of the story describing the dollhouse from Kezia's point of view is a verbal still life, with all the attention and care

that Mansfield could characteristically lavish on the miniature. One cannot help wondering how much Brett's picture had to do with prompting this story.[63]

Its child on the gate is a much more complex mixture of responses and initiatives than Pearl Button; the narrative method has 'that strange, perpetual weaving and unweaving' of the self that Pater describes. Its construction of a colonial situation is ambivalent. The colony has been tainted by the social hierarchies of the metropolitan centre, but the lamp remains as a bond between Kezia and her apparent other, Else. Mansfield's encounter with European art and writing enables her to hone her technique and realize that 'a young country is a real heritage, though it takes one time to recognise it. But New Zealand is in my very bones.'[64]

3
A Born Actress and Mimic: August 1908 – November 1911

> Would you not like to try *all* sorts of lives – one is so very small – but that is the satisfaction of writing – one can impersonate so many people – [1]

One of the last glimpses of Mansfield in New Zealand is an account of her attending a tea party held in her honour by the Prime Minister's wife, wearing a tweed suit with furs and what the local newspaper describes as a picturesque hat. She herself was critical of colonial fashion, including the hat, as she told her older sister:

> I've nothing fashionable *at all* – simplicity and art shades reign supreme – A black flop hat with a wide wreath of mauve chrysanthemums round the crown – a little evening frock of satin – soft satin – made exactly after the pattern of Grandmother Dyer's wedding dress…Clothes ought to be a joy to the artistic eye – a silent reflex of the soul.[2]

For the next three years, once she had arrived in London, she appeared in a series of startling disguises. When she met her first husband, George Bowden, he reports that she appeared demure; when they met again 'she was dressed "more or less Maori fashion," with some sort of scarf or kerchief over her shoulders, and there was "something almost eerie about it, as though of a psychic transformation"'.[3] Bowden's way of explaining this change to Alpers was to suggest that she had managed to enact her admiration of the Decadents, as he said that she looked like Oscar Wilde. He seems to have found her kaleidoscopic nature attractive, and so was perhaps prepared for the oddity of her clothes for her wedding to him: she was dressed entirely in black, wearing a shiny black hat as if she were at a funeral rather than a wedding. Her appearance was altered by seeing exhibitions of art and artefacts; the pink kimono that Orton remembers her wearing was the result of her attending a big Japanese exhibition in Shepherd's Bush in 1910. After her death, Virginia Woolf recalls that she 'had her look of a Japanese doll, with the fringe combed quite straight across her forehead'.[4] Implicit in these disguises, Maori, Japanese or cross-dressing, is an awareness of multiple selves, and perhaps of the difficulty of deciding what aspect of the 'soul' to reflect in one's clothes, since the changes of costume indicate ambivalence about race, gender and social position.

Brigid Brophy sees Mansfield's changes of costume as part of a response to rejection by her mother, whose many pregnancies were feared and resented:

> There is an evident difficulty, almost a formal conundrum, about a daughter's identifying herself with a mother who did not want to have her in the first place. The difficulty in identification made for an uncertainty in identity. Katherine Mansfield attested this by her experiments in personality and even by playing on the formal components of the very mark of identity, her name. The amateur 'cellist Kathleen Beauchamp did not change into the professional writer without trying a number of chrysalises, including the translation of Beauchamp into Schönfeld; she had already published several stories as Katherine Mansfield when she suddenly – and briefly – appeared as Katherina Mansfield. For personal use she had almost as many names as friends. Quite apart from her innumerable love-names with Murry, she ran, between various relationships and the mirror of her journal, a Joycean gamut of pseudonyms: – Kass, Kassie, Katie, K.T, Kath, Katya, Yékaterina.[5]

In her writing for journals she had a range of other pseudonyms: Julian Mark, Lili Heron, The Tiger, Boris Petrovsky, Elizabeth Stanley. Ida Baker is observant about a chameleon quality in Mansfield's clothes and appearance in her memoirs: 'She was a born actress and mimic, and even in her ordinary everyday life took colour from the company she was in.'[6] She reports that Mansfield, pregnant by Garnet Trowell, spent an enormous amount of money, 27 shillings, on a hat to wear for her reproachful mother's arrival in London in 1909. When Mrs Beauchamp saw her, she told her that she looked like an old woman, and made her give the hat to the chambermaid in the hotel where she was staying. The attempt at imitating colonial Wellington and dressing to gain parental approval had misfired.

Role-playing and theatrical control recur as themes in Mansfield's personal writing at this period. She writes to her lover, Trowell, that she wants to revolutionize the art of public recitation:

> A darkened stage – a great – high backed oak chair – flowers – shaded lights – a low table filled with curious books – and to wear a simple, beautifully coloured dress... *Tone* should be my secret... this is in my power because I know I possess the power of holding people.[7]

Using clothes to manipulate others, or to create a protective facade, is a motif in her stories: Laura's mother controls Laura's rebellion in 'The Garden-Party' by dropping an elegant black hat on her daughter's head (perhaps an oblique response to the humiliation of the expensive hat that Mansfield's mother despised), and Miss Brill's fur is a source of comfort and then humiliation. When Mansfield and William Orton were in a close relationship, she wrote herself into his journal, again providing herself with costumes, or a lack of them, for different roles. Whether the events she describes happened it is impossible to tell, but he quotes what she wrote:

> When the bells were striking five the Man came to see me. He gathered me up in his arms and carried me to the Black Bed. Very brown and strong was he... It drew dark. I crouched against him like a wild cat. Quite impersonally I admired my silver stockings bound beneath the knee with spiked ribbons, my yellow suède shoes fringed with white fur. How vicious I looked! We made love to each other like two wild beasts.[8]

Various discourses seem to intersect here. At first the woman seems the helpless victim of male passion, with an orientalist hint of racial otherness about the Man, but then she shows a voracious sexual appetite. She pauses, however, suspending her lust to admire in the tone of a fashion correspondent the appropriate animality of her outfit, with its spikes and fur; once she is sure that she is dressed for the part her carnal passion reasserts itself. The voyeurism directed mainly at the self is continued later in the passage, when either the Man or Michael, Orton's pseudonym, comes home with Catherine, who again sets the scene and controls the tone:

> I lit a candle – the world faded away. I acted. He tore my clothes from my shoulders. I laughed – bent forward – graceful and lithe – blew out the candle and stood naked to the waist in the moon-lit room … He knelt before me, his arms round my body. I crushed him against me – shook back my hair and laughed at the moon. I felt mad with passion – I wanted to kill.[9]

This carefully choreographed scene is full of clichés from the sensational fiction of the period, but with the protagonist rather than the narrator describing herself as 'graceful and lithe'; Mansfield had read the novels of Elinor Glyn and her influence is evident. 'I acted' seems to refer more to playing a formulaic part than to taking action. It is difficult to reconcile the narcissistic *femme fatale* of these passages with the woman John Middleton Murry met not long afterwards:

> She was ready to go out, dressed in a tailored suit of dark blue serge, with a small cream-coloured straw-hat trimmed with a tiny bunch of gay flowers – there was something almost boyish about her. Perhaps it came from the little tailored coat, which hung straight from the shoulders. But no: it was more inward than that. She was not, somehow, primarily a woman. I was not conscious of her as a woman. She was a perfectly exquisite, perfectly simple human being, whose naturalness made me natural. With her there was no need to pretend.[10]

The element of gender transgression is as evident in this passage as it is in Bowden's, but the reader who has read the previous passages is more likely to interpret the crisp boyishness of Mansfield's appearance in Murry's account as another act, the equivalent of a female actor playing Peter Pan, rather than an unaffected naturalness. It is not surprising, given the versatility shown by these changes of image, that Vera Brittain and Rebecca West remembered

Mansfield's appearance at a lesbian night club, The Cave of the Golden Calf, where she either introduced the acts or performed herself.[11] The disguises seem to be culturally constructed, multifarious responses to European artistic life, Maori history and bourgeois Wellington rather than 'a silent reflex of the soul'. This chapter traces the impact on Mansfield of the intellectual life in London of which she became a part before she met Murry, specifically the influence of A. R. Orage and the other writers connected with the *New Age*, and focuses particularly on three stories about gender relations within a family. These stories all use clothes as signifiers, and demonstrate that Mansfield had a range of fictional disguises early in her career which paralleled her changes of physical appearance.

Changes of mask are more evident at this stage of Mansfield's life than at any other. Her insecurity and excitement about being a colonial writer in the metropolis, an aesthete in a conservative society, and a bisexually active woman in a world in which women were expected be subservient in private and professional life, seemed to her to require protective disguises. Her valiant attempts to fulfil the injunctions that she had quoted from Oscar Wilde proved physically and emotionally disastrous. In pushing everything as far as it would go, she lost her chance of bearing children and exposed herself to the most prevalent European disease of the early twentieth century, tuberculosis. With uncanny accuracy, she had predicted, in her chubby and healthy youth in New Zealand: 'I shall end of course – by killing myself.'[12] After the seven-week voyage from New Zealand Mansfield arrived in London in August 1908 with an annual allowance from her father of £100. She re-established her relationship with the family of her cello teacher, Mr Trowell; his twin sons were musicians and Mansfield began a love affair with one of them, Garnet. It is clear from her letters that she wanted and expected to marry him, but she fell out with his parents. She became pregnant by him in the spring of 1909, and at the same time married George Bowden but left him immediately. Her mother came to London, having been informed of her daughter's marriage and the disgrace that her scandalous conduct was bringing on the family name, and took her to a pension in Bavaria where she left her; by this time Trowell had cut himself off from her. Mansfield had a miscarriage in June, and stayed in Bavaria until the end of the year because she was involved in a relationship with a Polish critic and translator Floryan Sobieniowski. They shared an enthusiasm for the poetry of Walt Whitman, and Sobieniowski probably introduced her to the work of Chekhov. He was also the most likely source of her infection with gonorrhoea, which proved fatal to her. Claire Tomalin's account of the disease[13] explains that its symptoms were obvious in men but could be ignored in women, and the medical expectation was that female infection would only occur in prostitutes. If the gonococci entered the patient's bloodstream, the disease became systemic and could cause infertility, arthritis, inflammation of the heart and pleurisy. Mansfield developed all these conditions because, having returned to Britain in January, she had an operation in March 1910 in which her left fallopian tube was removed as it was infected with gonococci; her surgery enabled the infection to spread to her other organs. She only knew for certain what had happened when Dr Sorapure explained it to her in 1918, though Tomalin speculates that long before this she must have had some idea about the cause of her recurrent illnesses. From 1910 onwards she was never in good health; gonorrhoea does not directly cause tuberculosis but the bacillus can establish itself easily in a body weakened by disease, malnutrition or privation.

Ida Baker began to act consistently as nurse, housekeeper, confidante and friend to Mansfield from the time of her operation, though they did not always live together. Baker recognized the significance that Mansfield attached to her freedom to write. In February 1910 her first story, 'The Child-Who-Was-Tired', was published in the *New Age*, where she also published the stories that were collected in *In a German Pension* which appeared in December 1911. She became part of Orage's circle of friends, living with him and his partner Beatrice Hastings for a while. When she moved to a flat on her own in Chelsea she had a relationship with William Orton, and possibly with others in the *New Age* group; she was also actively engaged in London's cultural life, and specifically she saw the Japanese exhibition and Fry's 'Manet and the Post-Impressionists' in 1910. She found the *New Age* group congenial and fun; they met in the ABC tearooms in Chancery Lane on Tuesday afternoons to smoke and talk about *No Wage*, as Orage ruefully called the journal. In May 1911 the Beauchamp family arrived from New Zealand for the coronation of George V, though Harold Beauchamp was detained on bank business and missed it. Mansfield produced a

pastiche of the fifteenth idyll of Theocritus for the *New Age* satiriz-
ing the coronation;[14] her brother Leslie was excited by what he saw
as her growing reputation in the literary world, and the brother and
sister became increasingly close.

During these years Mansfield shows, as with the skit on
Theocritus, how effectively she can borrow others' clothes. For the
New Age she and Beatrice Hastings produced a series of lively parodies; several of them involve sexual encounters. The landscape in
the parody of Eden Philpotts' fiction is a preparation for his meeting
with a woman (the ellipses are part of the text):

> [T]he signpost white and stark on the road below the red-roofed
> farm led the eye towards Burryzizzer, lying like a maid amid the
> heather … the meaning of the familiar and yet … I saw a gleam of
> rounded whiteness … nay, creamness, milkness … something – a
> sensation of approaching primevalness.[15]

In the parody of H. G. Wells's *Ann Veronica* the prose is less ornate:
'So we stowed Biology and got to business' is repeated three times.[16]
The skit on Arnold Bennett's prose reveals the parodist's attitude to
inclusive realism:

> In Pottinghame High Street, at seventeen minutes past three on a
> certain Sunday in the year of our Lord eighteen hundred and
> ninety-five, the fine dust was stirring. It was round, grey, pierc-
> ing, sandy dust that rose and fell with precocious senility; for the
> month was June, and June is early for dust.[17]

A less happy instance of Mansfield mimicking another writer
occurred in relation to her first story to be published in the *New Age*,
'The Child-Who-Was-Tired'. Elisabeth Schneider observes in an article for *Modern Language Notes* in 1935[18] that the story seems to be an
unacknowledged imitation of Chekhov's 'Sleepy'; Schneider assumes
that it was not deliberate plagiarism but an unconscious memory.
The debate was taken up in an acrimonious correspondence in
the *Times Literary Supplement* in 1951 which is reproduced in an
appendix to Tomalin's biography; Tomalin herself considers that the
'story is drawn directly or indirectly from a specific Chekhov story,
and should properly be described as a free translation'[19] and, of
course, acknowledged, which it was not. She suggests that it was this

shadow of plagiarism that enabled Sobieniowski to blackmail Mansfield in 1920. She paid him £40 to recover some of her letters; as Tomalin observes, it is unlikely that she would be worried about

> a long-extinct love-affair...It is perhaps more likely that something in them threatened to damage her professional reputation: and the most likely area might be the references to her old plagiarism of Chekhov's *'Spat' khochetsia'*, 'The Child-Who-Was-Tired' in her version.[20]

At the same time as she was exercising her talent for mimicry, either as parody or partial plagiarism, Mansfield was exploring other aspects of the self which involved dressing it in different clothes, looking at it in different lights, and examining its mirror images. A story called 'His Sister's Keeper' was among the unbound papers that Murry inherited at Mansfield's death. It was not published until 1997, when it was included as an appendix in Pamela Dunbar's *Radical Mansfield*, and it is included in the *Notebooks*. It is dated 1909; Margaret Scott's footnote comments that it is of interest because it shows Mansfield's 'idealised and romantic view of her young brother expressed six years *before* his death'.[21] This view presupposes that the reader will identify Mansfield with only one of the characters in the story, the unnamed 'girl', whereas a reading of the whole story suggests that women who take an idealized and romantic view are allowing themselves to be written by the scripts of their society, and that the idealized and romantic is only one facet of a much darker aspect of the psyche. The story manipulates the reader's recognition of narrative clichés, setting up the opposition of the innocent good girl and the experienced bad girl, only to undermine it and show them as doubles, mirror images. An unnamed girl leaves an overnight ferry in Dieppe and boards a train. She is alone in a compartment until, at the last moment, another woman, called Lily but always referred to as the Fellow Passenger, joins her. The Fellow Passenger is heavily made-up, and wearing scarlet; she preens while the girl takes out a copy of *A Shropshire Lad*. The girl falls asleep while the Fellow Passenger reads her book; when she wakes the Fellow Passenger asks her about the photograph pasted in the book. Prompted by this, the girl describes her intense love for her innocent, idealistic younger brother, and is surprised to find the

Fellow Passenger in tears. She explains that she too had such a brother, a twin. She lived in the country while he shared a flat in London; when she was a young girl, she went from the country to visit an aunt in London. Her train was late; when she arrived her aunt was nowhere to be seen but a woman pretending to be the aunt's maid took her off in a cab to what proved to be a strange house, and locked her into a bedroom. She awoke to find that she was being caressed in the dark by a man who proved to be her brother. Both were horrified when she struggled and turned on the light, and they separated. As the Fellow Passenger finishes her story, which the girl defines to herself as a 'strange, terrible dream', they arrive at their destination, which may be Paris but remains unspecific. The Fellow Passenger greets the man who is waiting for her gaily, but the girl rushes past the man who comes to meet her.

Because of the constant parallels that are drawn between them, and the fact that the girl is not named, the two young women seem to be two aspects of one self. One of Freud's instances of perceiving the self as other, in his essay 'The Uncanny', is his own glimpse of his reflection in a train, which he does not recognize as himself until he stands up: 'I at once realized to my dismay that the intruder was nothing but my own reflection in the looking-glass on the open door. I can still recollect that I thoroughly disliked his appearance.'[22] The Fellow Passenger seems to represent the unrecognized, repressed side of the respectable girl, who shows fear in her presence: ' "Hallo" said the Fellow Passenger, "got a fit of the taradiddles – your hands are on the jump" ' (230). Julia Kristeva interprets the recognition of something that has come into the open but should have remained secret in this way: 'The foreigner is within us. And when we flee from or struggle against the foreigner, we are fighting our unconscious – that "improper" facet of our impossible "own and proper." '[23] In Mansfield's story each girl appears to be the other's foreigner. The story pivots on the juxtaposed versions of much-loved brothers in which the second seems to rewrite the first, but the sinister suggestion of menace beneath an innocent exterior is present from the beginning. The title, 'His Sister's Keeper', gestures towards male authority over a reluctant woman, either mad or imprisoned. It echoes Cain's impatient response to God in Genesis: 'And the Lord said unto Cain, Where is Abel thy brother? And he said, I know not: am I my brother's keeper?'[24] It is the twin whose sister trusts 'his high ideals – his reverence for women' (233), who appears to be her protector yet attempts to rape her, and would have done so had she not turned on the light. Though he does not know that his victim is his sister, the scene forms a macabre parallel to the other girl's account of life with her brother:

> 'And at night after he had gone to bed we had a mysterious game called "Pyjama arm". I used to go in the dark and lie down on his bed, my head pillowed on his arm while he told me all his thoughts, his growing ideas, his strange little fantastic conceptions'.
>
> (231)

Perhaps he did not tell all his little fantasies, and she apparently told none of hers.

When the girl lands in France at three in the morning at the beginning of the story her tense mental state is conveyed since she finds 'Dieppe like the mouth of some giant monster' (228). The train journey takes place at night; the girl's perspective seems to heighten ordinary events to violence: 'A porter ran along smashing up the darkness with a jangling bell' (229). She seems to be trying to repress her own awareness of what she has done. This is suggested by the ellipses in the text:

> Three o'clock in the morning … and Dieppe … when she had only made up her mind at six o'clock the evening before, and at seven she had been at Victoria, debating still, still safe, and now … well, anything to live.
>
> (229)

The nature of her insecurity is implied when she looks half-sneeringly at the wedding-ring on the finger of a newly married woman who is with her husband: 'They looked ridiculous – abashed, self-conscious and almost apologetic towards the waiter. Heaven preserve her!' The exclamation seems to refer to her own wish to escape bourgeois marriage, but the text is fissured with ambiguities.

When the two young women settle in their compartment, they are both armed with male-authored texts. The girl lends *A Shropshire Lad* to her companion; its significance is not made explicit but its thematic preoccupation with doomed youth and betrayal of innocence has an oblique relevance to the story. One of the poems, 'With Rue My Heart Is Laden', contains the lines: 'The rose-lipt girls are sleeping / In fields where roses fade.'[25] In return for Housman, the Fellow Passenger offers the girl a brisk near-quotation from

Shakespeare's *King John*: 'Gilding refined gold and painting the lily' (229).[26] She acknowledges that she is contravening this male authority by applying face-powder recklessly but 'lilies have no right to go journeying in railway carriages, my dear'. She is, in every sense, a scarlet woman: her coat and bag are scarlet, her face is covered with rouge, and she laughs 'showing her little white teeth like seeds in a red fruit'(229). The discrepancy between this and the connotations of her name, purity and death, is one of the story's disturbing disjunctions. She writes two scripts for her companion based on her innocent appearance, assuming that she herself is covering up a sexual liaison by pretending to visit a relation, while the girl is really visiting her grandmother:

> 'What are you reading... Oh, don't tell me, it's poems. And you wanted to be alone in the carriage, to curl up and look out of the window, then read a little verse, then remember how he smiled at you in the last verse of the hymn on Sunday evening. It's a good thing that I came in to chaperon you... you're too pretty for empty railway carriages. Are you going to stay in Paris with grandma in rooms conveniently near the Louvre. I am.'

(230)

As soon as the girl speaks Lily realizes that she is not with an infatuated *ingénue*; both women are involved in taking some kind of sexual risk. The irony of her other supposition, of the value of her own role as chaperone, is that she is at least as dangerous as a travelling companion to the girl as a predatory man in that she represents the fears that the girl is trying to protect herself from; in fact the Fellow Passenger brings to light what the girl is attempting to repress.

The Fellow Passenger has a mask, which the girl finds enviable: 'her assurance, her laughter, the very way she powdered her face, all seemed to speak of success and experience' (230). Their journey together in the dark becomes a psychological rather than a physical adventure: 'She could not quite see the future. Felt suddenly that she had plunged into a sea without the slightest idea as to whether she was swimming towards land or quicksand, or mirage' (230). It is not a one-way process. The Fellow Passenger is moved by the girl's devotion to her brother, though there is a constant implication of an unacknowledged incestuous response to him; when the girl says that the photograph is of her brother a 'wave of colour seemed to flood over her whole body' (230). The Fellow Passenger's narrative is formulaic in that girls being tricked into prostitution is a staple of Victorian and Edwardian sensational writing; she acknowledges it when she says: 'Stories I had overheard from the servants, newspaper reports that I had half read, vague transitory thoughts I had imagined almost obliterated – they trooped before me now' (233). This may partially refer back to an early part of her narrative, when she says that: 'We decided that when I was old enough we should live together. I did not wish to marry, he filled my life, and I was sound asleep, really, you know' (232). One story overlays another: like the girl, who actually sleeps in the course of the story, the Fellow Passenger conceals her taboo desire for her brother, but the sensational sequence of events in her narrative forces her to confront it. The implicit outcome is that, in recognizing her own guilt, she takes to another forbidden style of life and becomes a prostitute: 'We both left that room, but I went into another' (233). When the train arrives, the Fellow Passenger resumes her mask and drops the handkerchief which is sodden with her tears, but the girl seems to have changed: 'A man came up to her gladly, quickly, but she almost ran past him and out alone into the street' (234). Mansfield was of course familiar with Wilde's *The Picture of Dorian Gray* and Robert Louis Stevenson's *Dr Jekyll and Mr Hyde*, but the exploration of the divided self in 'His Sister's Keeper' is distinctive in that the girl and the Fellow Passenger overlap and blur into one another. When the girl comments that the Fellow Passenger's story, related as actual experience, is a 'strange, terrible dream' she seems to be hinting that she knows how repressed incestuous desires reveal themselves; the doubling in the story resembles the relationship between the captain and his mysterious guest in Joseph Conrad's 'The Secret Sharer', particularly because of the insistent repetition of the phrase 'the Fellow Traveller'. Mansfield was probably only 20 when she wrote it; it is a much more complex story, stylistically and thematically, in its unravelling of role-playing and masks than the stories she wrote for the *New Age*.

When she was very ill and no longer able to work as a reviewer, Mansfield wrote to Orage, the editor of the *New Age*, about his

wonderful unfailing kindness to me in the 'old days'…you taught me to write, you taught me to think…I cannot tell you how often I call to mind your conversation or how often, in *writing*, I remember my master.[27]

Orage, whom T. S. Eliot regarded as the best literary critic of his period in London, recognized the quality of Mansfield's writing as soon as she submitted a story to him in 1910. He edited the *New Age* from 1908 until 1922; Bernard Shaw, H. G. Wells, Hilaire Belloc, Arnold Bennett and G. K. Chesterton were regular contributors in the first phase of his editorship, and he also published, when they were unknown, Ezra Pound, Wyndham Lewis, Edwin Muir and Herbert Read. The *New Age* group provided Mansfield with the intellectual and artistic stimulus she was looking for; it was the first Socialist weekly in London and was alert to radical experiments in the art, politics and culture of its time. It reproduced work by Epstein, Gaudier-Brzeska, Wyndham Lewis and Picasso, and encouraged debate about current issues. Arnold Bennett, for example, in reviewing 'Manet and the Post-Impressionists', draws a revealing parallel between the visual arts and literature:

> The average critic always calls me, both in praise and dispraise, 'photographic'; and I always rebut the epithet with disdain, because in the sense meant by the average critic I am not photographic. But supposing that in a deeper sense I were? Supposing a young writer turned up and forced me, and some of my contemporaries – us who fancy ourselves a bit – to admit that we had been concerning ourselves unduly with [in]essentials, that we had been worrying ourselves to achieve infantile realisms? Well, that day would be a great and disturbing day – for us. And we should see what we should see.[28]

Young writers such as Mansfield had already turned up to parody him, and would within the next few years disturb Bennett's fictional techniques; Virginia Woolf's essay 'Mr Bennett and Mrs Brown', published in 1919, accuses Bennett precisely of putting infantile realism in the place of the multifarious shifts of an ordinary mind on an ordinary day. Similarly Pound, writing about Imagism in 1911, describes as a method for poetry a technique that Mansfield perfected: 'The artist seeks out the luminous detail and presents it. He does not comment.'[29]

Orage's own radicalism is evident in his little book *Friedrich Nietzsche: The Dionysian Spirit of the Age*, published in 1906. It is evident from the aphorisms he quotes approvingly that Mansfield must have found him intellectually sympathetic: 'Write with blood, and then thou wilt learn that blood is spirit';[30] 'The secret of a joyful life is to live dangerously';[31] 'All that is done for love is done beyond good and evil.'[32] The relativism that Mansfield was already exploring in her writing, for instance in her comparison of Maori and pakeha cultures, is expressed by Orage:

> But the comparative study of moralities begun by Nietzsche already begins to demonstrate the fact that there is in reality no absolute Good, no absolute Evil. Of nothing is it any longer possible to say: This is Good everywhere and always; that is Bad everywhere and always. Good and Bad must be determined on every occasion afresh, and always in relation to a definite purpose, by which alone anything can be either good or bad.[33]

Bergson was also championed by the *New Age*, and M. D. Eder introduced psychoanalysis to *New Age* readers long before the wider British public became aware of it. The *New Age* published translation of works by Chekhov and Dostoevsky; Arnold Bennett discussed their work in his influential weekly literary column. Duckworth published two volumes of Chekhov's stories in translation, one in 1903 and the next in 1908; Bennett wrote in the *New Age* in 1909:

> Beneath the outward simplicity of his work is concealed the most wondrous artifice, the artifice that is embedded deep in nearly all great art. All we English novelists ought to study *The Kiss* and *The Black Monk* ... We have no writer, and we never have had one, nor has France, who could mould the material of life, without distorting it, into such complex form to such an end of beauty.[34]

Mansfield shared this view though she may not have read the article. She wrote to Koteliansky in 1919 that Chekhov's letter

> about the duty of the artist to *put* the 'question' – not to solve it but so to put it that one is completely satisfied seems to me one of the most valuable things I have ever read. It opens – it discovers rather, a new world.[35]

The element of political awareness that had been a recurrent strand in her early writing about New Zealand becomes evident in what she writes in Europe at this time. Before she met Orage and the *New Age* contributors she had written a poem that anticipates the memorable scene in *Mrs Dalloway* in which an old crone sings a love song outside Regent's Park tube station. In 'The Trio' two women and a man, withered and cold, stand outside a warehouse:

> Then, at a signal from the draggled man
> The women sing – God, from their withered mouths
> A tragedy of singing issues forth
> High pitched and wandering, crazy tuneless tunes
> Over and over comes the same refrain
> 'Say, shepherds, have you seen my Flora pass this way.'[36]

The grotesque discrepancy between the situation of the dispossessed singers and the song, evoking Merrie England, has an ironically political thrust that becomes increasingly evident as she writes for the *New Age*. She wrote a letter which was published there on 11 August 1910 in response to press treatment of the murderer Dr Crippen, who tried to escape to America with his lover who was dressed as a boy. He was captured as a result of a technological innovation; a marconigram was sent by the captain of the ship to Scotland Yard. Mansfield's argument is that the case was pre-judged through its treatment by the press:

> There can be no question of judging Crippen. He can be bought outright, with a photograph and a book of words, by any street gamin possessed of a halfpenny.
>   Surely we owe a debt of gratitude to all concerned who have shepherded us in this personally conducted tour into the hidden chambers of that machine which separates the wheat from the tares with all the impartiality and infallibility of our Courts of Law.[37]

Two weeks later another letter from her on a public issue appeared, but this time she is disguised as 'a respectable citizeness of pagan England'.[38] She specifically disowns her own colonial past to sneer at two Canadian novelists, Elinor Glyn and Grant Allen:

> If Elinor Glyn is the prophetic woman's voice crying out of the wilderness of Canadian literature, let her European sister

novelists lift shekelled hands in prayer that the 'great gulf' may ever yawn more widely.[39]

'Shekelled' is puzzling, as no such word exists. It combines the sound of 'shackled' with the meaning associated with 'shekels', which is a colloquialism for ready cash. Its sense remains obscure. The reader would probably not guess that the snobbish tone about the colonies in this passage is adopted by a New Zealander; Americans are treated with similar condescension: 'your companion on the Elevated Railway may be hiding under a striped chewing-gum wrapper the quivering first fruits of his soul.'[40] There is a metropolitan tone to this letter that is as affected as she seems in Frank Swinnerton's first memory of her, a year or two later:

> My eyes were chiefly occupied with Katherine Mansfield, a slight, trim girl with very dark hair combed straight down over her brow, who sat on the floor, or a hassock, with quite oriental stillness. She spoke in a murmur. She said, from between almost closed lips: 'One doesn't know whether to have dozens of children, or devote oneself altogether to art.' I forget what I advised in this curious dilemma.[41]

She was to satirize striking a pose of this kind in her later fiction, for example in 'Bliss' and the painful 'Marriage à la Mode'. Although the stories that she wrote for the *New Age* were satirical, like the letters, they mostly also fit predictably into the kinds of national stereotypes that link Americans with chewing-gum. The Bavarians in these stories, which were collected and published by Stephen Swift as *In a German Pension*, are mostly brutishly physical, obsessed by their digestive systems and by rigid patterns of etiquette. The narrator is a foreign woman who often participates in the action. Mansfield explains the impetus for these stories in a letter to Murry written in 1918, several years after she wrote them:

> Ive two 'kick-offs' in the writing game. *One* is joy…The other 'kick off' is my old original one, and (had I not known love) it would have been my all. Not hate or destruction…but an *extremely* deep sense of hopelessness – of everything doomed to disaster – almost wilfully, stupidly … *a cry against corruption* that is *absolutely* the nail on the head.[42]

Alpers records that Mansfield used illustrations from a popular German review called *Die Jugend* as a trigger for her sketches for the *New Age*; *Jugendstil* was the German version of the English Arts and Crafts movement that spread to France as Art Nouveau. Her interest in this form of visual art was in the satirical bite of its caricatures and cartoons, their cries against corruption, but in some of her *New Age* stories she moves beyond lively sketching to a more textured fiction. The plot of 'Frau Brechenmacher Attends a Wedding' is almost encompassed by its title; the frau is a young woman, the mother of five very small children. She and her husband, a postman, attend a wedding in their town, and return home when the festivities are over. The butt of the overt satire is Herr Brechenmacher:

> Herr Brechenmacher, completely overawed by this grand manner, so far forgot his rights as a husband as to beg his wife's pardon for jostling her against the banisters in his efforts to get ahead of everybody else.[43]

The brutal, beer-swilling patriarch's behaviour conforms to the caricature, but the story is written from his wife's perspective. Attending a wedding allows the young woman to reflect on her own situation, which she is mostly far too busy to do. At first the reader is invited to see her ironically; dressing in the dark passage to give her husband plenty of space in the lighted kitchen, she 'fastened her handkerchief round her neck with a beautiful brooch that had four medals to the Virgin dangling from it' (705). The naiveté of her admiration of the brooch indicates that she has accepted the prescribed role of faithful wife and mother, and is a willing doormat, to be trampled under male feet. She is humiliated to discover a discrepancy between what she feels and how she looks at the wedding; she 'seemed to fill out and become rosy and warm' (707) but she is mocked because the tape from her petticoat shows as she could not see what she was doing when she dressed. She sees what a dutiful wife might be expected to see when she arrives at the celebration, but when she looks at the bride she has 'the appearance of an iced cake all ready to be cut and served in neat little pieces to the bridegroom' (706). The narrative perspective modulates in and out of Frau Brechenmacher's vision, but the overall impression is that the text sees as she sees, and what she perceives here is violent. The bride is not a virgin: her daughter sits beside her wearing a wreath of forget-me-nots, a comment on the bride's inability to escape her situation. The head jailer is her mother, who has got the priest to force the reluctant woman into the marriage:

> She never took her eyes off her daughter, but wrinkled her brown forehead like an old monkey, and nodded now and again very solemnly. Her hands shook as she raised her beer mug, and when she had drunk she spat on the floor and savagely wiped her mouth with her sleeve.
>
> (708)

She is behaving like the men in the story; throughout there is an implication that girls are taught gender roles in order to trap them into motherhood, which turns them into brutalized pieces of domestic machinery who collaborate in ensnaring the next generation of women. Frau Brechenmacher, watching the dancing, 'forgot her five babies and her man and felt almost like a girl again. The music sounded sad and sweet. Her roughened hands clasped and unclasped themselves in the folds of her skirt' (709). Her girlish enjoyment and suppressed longing for romance are ruined by her husband's vulgar speech about the bridal pair, and the suggestive way in which he hands over a coffee pot holding a baby's bottle and two dolls in cradles. The road on her way home reflects her position in the cold and calculating patriarchal society she inhabits, and she confronts the memory that she has been suppressing: 'White and forsaken lay the road from the railway station to their house – a cold rush of wind blew her hood from her face, and suddenly she remembered how they had come home together the first night' (710). Her husband indulges in unsentimental nostalgia about how he taught her a lesson on their wedding night, after she gave him 'a clout on the ear' (711). The bleakness of his wife's situation, and by implication of all the dutiful women in her society, is made clear in the closing lines of the story, as she re-enacts her wedding night: 'She lay down on the bed and put her arm across her face like a child who expected to be hurt as Herr Brechenmacher lurched in' (711). The image of the bride as a cake ready to be cut up and served to her husband is explained by this repressed memory. This cry against corruption is unlike the brisk satire of most of the other stories, and much closer to a deep sense of hopelessness. Mansfield was asked by Sadler in 1920 whether she would allow Constable to bring out a new edition of *In a German Pension* but she wrote to Murry saying that she could not consider it: 'It is far too *immature* & I don't even acknowledge it today. I mean I don't "hold" by it. I cant go foisting that kind of stuff on the public – *its not good enough.*'[44]

In 'His Sister's Keeper' the Fellow Passenger's clothes and make-up are used paradoxically; this Lily is also Rose Red, and the apparent contradiction implicates the other girl in the story and invites the reader to speculate. Clothes are used in the Bavarian stories in a more obvious, overtly satirical way, to attack patriarchy. The dispiriting image of the bride in Frau Brechenmacher's story, and the Frau's own appearance at the wedding with a grotesque brooch and trailing petticoat strings, are juxtaposed against her husband's confidence in his bursting blue uniform with buttons 'shining with an enthusiasm which nothing but official buttons could possibly possess' (705). An early story, written in 1910 or 1911 and published in *Rhythm* (October 1912), addresses directly the relationship between clothes and identity. 'New Dresses' is a New Zealand story which was included by Murry in *Something Childish* (1924); in the *Rhythm* version the story is clearly set in Wellington but the family's names are German: Anna and Andreas Binzer and their children Elena and Rosa. The story concerns two new green cashmere dresses made for Rose and Helen by their mother and grandmother. Helen tears hers the first time she wears it, when the local doctor is having Sunday lunch with the family; she hides it and gives it away, but the doctor finds it by chance, and returns it, mended, to the grandmother, to protect Helen from her parents' anger. The dress is the focus for a series of alternative identities within the family, unobtrusively revealing colonial, class and gender anxieties. The baby boy in the family is admired because he is fearless and thumps with a spoon on his high chair; his father says: 'Go it, old man. Tell mother boys like to kick up a row' (543). When his sisters appear in their new dresses their mother 'could not help thrilling, they looked so very superior' (543). She looks admiringly at her husband and daughters, and thinks she made the dresses for his sake: 'And she fully believed it' (544). Mrs Carsfield's self-deception, masking the self from the self, involves an ordinary domestic cruelty which is mercilessly revealed in Mansfield's stories of family life. She favours one daughter at the expense of the other because one colludes with her sense that the family is superior, and the other does not:

> '[Y]ou didn't see Helen's clothes when I took them off tonight. Black from head to foot after a week. And when I compared them before her eyes with Rose's she merely shrugged, you know that habit she's got, and began stuttering.'
>
> (538)

The narrator later mentions in passing that Mrs Carsfield 'shrugged her shoulders in the way that her little daughter had caught from her' (540); imitation and a stutter suggest to the reader, though not to the mother, that the child may want approval, and may be silenced by her awareness that she cannot gain it.

Helen confides in the doctor, who thinks that the favourite, Rose, blushing in approved feminine fashion in her green dress, looks 'like a tomato in a lettuce salad' (544). Helen's insight into her mother's values is astute, and it confuses her own pleasure in the new dress. When the doctor asks her if she likes it, she replies: ' "Oh yes, I'd like to be born and die in it. But it was such a fuss – tryings on, you know, and pullings, and 'don'ts.' I believe mother would kill me if it got hurt" ' (545). Her language makes clear that she understands how her mother treasures the dresses as if they were animate beings and is savage in her defence of the family's status. The formal grammar of the story alters to indicate a shift to Helen's perspective; what she shows is a freedom that would be approved in her brother but is regarded as reprehensible in her. She works herself high on the swing, wondering whether the doctor's dog has finished its bones:

> Decided to go and see. Slower she swung, then took a flying leap; her tight skirt caught on a nail – there was a sharp, tearing sound – quickly she glanced at the others – they had not noticed – and then at the frock – at a hole big enough to stick her hand through.
>
> (545)

She hides the torn dress and lies to cover her tracks, but is promised a whipping by her father. The fact that it is the doctor who rescues her hints at a link between them that separates them from the other members of their colonial society. Helen is a reader, like the doctor; he quotes from *Hamlet*, 'Oh my prophetic soul!' (545) and, when the narrative is adopting his voice, there is a reference to Browning, 'he smelt a rat – smelt a Hamelin tribe of them' (546). The child, however, is conscious of her own play-acting: 'now and again she wanted to shout "I tore it, I tore it," and she fancied she had said it and seen their faces' (547). She wants to remove her own mask and theirs, but has learnt very early on that roles and disguises are part of domestic life.

This exploration of the hypocrisies of the Empire City is more subtly nuanced than Mansfield's early skits on British life, but they too investigate the significance of image, this time in public life. In a parody that mocks the British attitude to empire and gender, Mansfield and Beatrice Hastings satirize the role of the Poet Laureate by mimicking Alfred Austin on the coronation of George V:

> Droop ye no more – ye stalwart oaken trees,
> For mourning time is spent and put away –
> Red, white and blue unfurls, the morning breeze
> Brings leaves – strew leaves for Coronation Day.
> And thrill along your mighty, crusted bark,
> King George, our Sailor King, goes to be crowned,
> Your limbs have nursed his navy – the long mark
> Of his wide Empire by your arms is bound.
> Bud roses! scatter at the matron feet
> Of his proud consort, Mary, all your bloom.
> Let Englishman the bronzed Colonial meet
> In brotherhood – and weave upon the loom
> Of this great Empire stronger, deeper ties –
> Ties that shall hold 11,000 miles.
> Perhaps in some far Heaven of the skies
> Edward the Peace-maker looks down and smiles.[45]

The gap between myths of nationhood and reality is exposed in the image of the old roué Edward VII, renowned for his passion for racing and women rather than diplomacy, caricatured as Edward the Peace-maker, a bearded figure smiling down from a cloud like God the Father. The 'bronzed colonial' is an equally empty cliché, jumbled as it is with hearts of oak and mixed metaphors.

In her parodies, Mansfield shows her ability to mimic. C. K. Stead sees her skill in changing masks and assuming identities, in her letters as well as her personal behaviour, as indivisible from her fiction:

> This easy adoption of different masks, different voices, is one of the principal skills on which her success as a fiction writer rests, and it is not surprising to notice the way her recognition of the distinct character of each of her friends determines the persona she adopts in writing to them.[46]

Her experiments, both personal and literary, in impersonation and disguises between 1908 and 1911 caused lasting damage to her health, but prepared her to recognize the significance of the *Rhythm* group when she met them in 1912.

4
The Tiger: December 1911 – October 1915

MARCH
19 THURSDAY Dreamed about N. Z. Very delightful.
20 FRIDAY Dreamed about N. Z. again – one of the painful
dreams when Im there & hazy about my return ticket.[1]

The diary entry for 20 March 1914 comments with wry irony on the enthusiasm of the previous day. After she met the *New Age* group, Mansfield continued to write about New Zealand, but she did not want to live there; until her brother's death in October 1915 she felt exhilarated by being one of the European 'neo-barbarians' whose artistic innovations were shocking the establishment. There is less nostalgia for New Zealand in her personal writing at this period than at any other time, though her poems hint at a conscious effort to suppress memories of a geographically and culturally distant place. Many of her pieces in the *New Age* and in *Rhythm* were published under pseudonyms but in *Rhythm* in March 1913 she published under her own name a poem, 'Sea Song', which begins with the assertion that 'Memory dwells in my far away home, / She has nothing to do with me.' However, by the end of the poem, Memory, personified as an old woman, has been described in great detail searching for something lost, suggesting that the irretrievable world of childhood in New Zealand haunts the writer. When Memory 'Wails in my far away home' she is all too audible, although the night, like the poet, 'bids her be silent, / And bids her be still'.[2] When Leslie Beauchamp was killed, Memory's 'crazy song' had to be heard, partly as personal therapy, but until then Mansfield's creative energies were mainly occupied elsewhere.

A series of meetings took place in 1911 and 1912 that were definitively to alter Mansfield's life and writing. This chapter focuses on their significance for her, specifically on the effect on her writing of her close involvement with the *Rhythm* group of painters and writers. The first of the series of meetings has been described by the two men involved, whose memories were equally unreliable. The facts are therefore blurred, but the intellectual and artistic impact of the encounter is not. The first account is from J. D. Fergusson, who had settled in Paris in 1907; there he felt he had 'everything a young painter could want'.[3] He loved the Café d'Harcourt which was not considered respectable but had a lively Hungarian band, and was full of girls wearing daring clothes who worked for dressmakers and milliners. He went there with Anne Estelle Rice, the American painter:

> 'Well, one night my artist friend and I sat beside a very good-looking lad with a nice girl – they were apparently and quite rightly pleased with each other. We were sketching people round while they were beside us, so neither looked at them nor heard what they were saying, but I remembered the lad vaguely and with sympathy.'[4]

The lad had also noticed him; he was John Middleton Murry, and was, by his own account 'at a positive nadir of glumness' over the antics of his female companion, Yvonne, whose behaviour was 'intolerable; particularly intolerable, because I liked the look of this Englishman, with his rakish bowler-hat, his blue collar, his keen shaven face, and his fresh bow-tie'.[5] Murry says that they had a conversation:

> I found myself plunged into an exposition of Bergson's distinction between Time and Duration. My neighbour was not an Englishman, after all, but a Scot: and a painter to boot. His companion was a buxom and charming woman, with a fresh complexion, and smiling eyes of periwinkle blue: she was an American painter.[6]

Murry's version concludes with an invitation from the Scottish painter to visit his studio, but Murry characteristically lost the address that he was given.

Murry's father was a civil service clerk who was determined that his son should be sufficiently well-educated to move up the social scale; through charitable scholarships Murry went first to the Bluecoat School, Christ's Hospital, and then to Brasenose College, Oxford. He felt socially uneasy in both places, and escaped to Paris before he had completed his degree, reading the work of the philosopher Henri Bergson who was lecturing at this time at the Sorbonne. When he eventually visited it, the sense of security Murry felt in Fergusson's ordered and beautiful studio, being fed bread and butter and called 'Murry, lad', was almost unique in his experience, as was Fergusson's idea of an artist as being anyone who resisted mechanical uniformity. Murry himself preferred Fergusson's earlier work, its muted palette showing the influence of Whistler, to his Fauvist paintings, so he was all the more impressed by Fergusson's recognition that his new style was less appealing to the public, and by his uncommercial attitude to his work:

> If he stuck to his guns, and faced without flinching the unpopu-
> larity he knew was coming to him through abandoning his
> earlier and very saleable manner, he was, in his function of
> advance-guard, somehow clearing the way for future freedom for
> the tribe. Again, it followed that it was unseemly for an artist to
> live uncleanly or in disorder: he must embody a natural disci-
> pline of his own. His rhythm must be his own rhythm: but
> rhythm he must have. In other words, art was not a profession.
> No man could be a professional artist. By profession he might be
> a painter, a writer, or equally well a boxer or a bootblack; whether
> he was an artist or not depended on what he was in himself. Art
> was a quality of being – an achievement of, or an effort towards
> integrity.[7]

Fergusson did not articulate these views in so many words, but his way of living expressed them; he was 15 years older than Murry and was clear about his artistic and human priorities. He taught at the Academie de la Palette and exhibited at the Salon d'Automne. The Salon had been established in 1903 'in opposition to the restrictive policies of the official Salons';[8] in the introductory essay to the 1905 catalogue, the artistic aesthetic described by the painter Elie Faure anticipates the preoccupations of *Rhythm*. A Bergsonian emphasis on heterogeneity rather than homogeneity is evident in his celebration of the new Salon:

> Le Salon d'Automne has done away with the barrenness of categories. It is like a spiritual garden in which all the flowers mixed together have a natural harmony. This is the harmony which light, space and the secret rhythm of things imposes on the road, the moving sky, the monotonous plains, the sea, crowds and solitude. Every work of art and every group of works should be the universe in microcosm. The 'genre' here is unknown, it is the confused order of life itself.[9]

The Salon was very selective and uncompromising; it encouraged the work of the Fauves. Fergusson felt released from the constraints of the Royal Scottish Academy, especially when he was made a *sociétaire* of the Salon:

> 'To me, considering myself a revolutionary, this was a very great honour … it had the effect of confirming my feeling of independence, the greatest thing in the world, not merely in art but in everything.'[10]

He frequented the café in Montparnasse called La Closerie des Lilas as well as the Café d'Harcourt, and knew Picasso and the artists and writers associated with the Symbolist and Cubist movements who met there. Murry was more intellectual and philosophical than Fergusson, but he describes himself as being 'enriched' by their contact:

> One word was recurrent in all our strange discussions – the word 'rhythm'. We never made any attempt to define it; nor even took any precaution to discover whether it had the same significance for us both … For F— it was the essential quality in a painting or a sculpture; and since it was at that moment that the Russian Ballet first came to Western Europe for a season at the Châtelet, dancing was obviously linked, by rhythm, with the plastic arts. From that it was but a short step to the position that rhythm was the

distinctive element in all the arts, and that the real purpose of 'this modern movement' – a phrase frequent on F—'s lips – was to reassert the pre-eminence of rhythm.[11]

As a result of this encounter, Murry involved his friends from Oxford, Michael Sadler[12] and Frederick Goodyear, in founding the magazine *Rhythm*, with Fergusson as its art editor. Fergusson comments:

> 'I adapted my picture to make a cover. My only condition was that it would be cheap, not a de luxe magazine. I wanted any herd boy to be able to have the latest information about modern painting from Paris.'[13]

There were articles in French and English, and one of Murry's pieces contains a paragraph of untranslated Italian,[14] so the herd boys would have required linguistic skills, but the condition was met, and the first issue of *Rhythm* appeared in the summer of 1911:

> It was the first magazine of the pre-war years to identify itself with the spirit of change intimated in Fry's Post-Impressionist exhibition; with its bold layout and numerous illustrations, it constituted in itself an artistic statement … and it stressed – unusually among contemporary journals of its type – the interdependence of the arts, their common ideals and organisational principles.[15]

Six months after the launch of *Rhythm*, Katherine Mansfield's *In a German Pension* was equivocally reviewed in the *New Age*: she was accused of 'lachrymose sentimentality' and described dismissively as 'a sketch artist, and very expert in producing vignettes that contain every necessary detail, if sometimes more than is necessary'.[16] She had been parodied in the *New Age*, and 'a little *symboliste* prose-poem of hers called "Along the Gray's Inn Road" had been made to look absurd by appearing among the Letters to the Editor with a "Sir" in front of it'.[17] She was therefore interested in finding a new outlet for her work and tried *Rhythm*; she sent Murry a fey story which he rejected, but when she offered him 'The Woman at the Store' he accepted it enthusiastically and became anxious to meet her. They met in December 1911, the second in this sequence of meetings; in April 1912 Murry became her lodger and then her lover. She is named as the assistant editor of *Rhythm* in the issue for June 1912. Murry describes the third in the series of crucial encounters, this time between Mansfield and Fergusson:

> I wanted Katherine to meet my hero, F—, and I wanted him to give us his blessing. He did so with a will: he put his hand on my shoulder with a smile, while Katherine was looking out of his studio window. 'Well, Murry lad, you know my views about marriage and this art-business; but if ever a couple ought to be together, it's you two.' No doubt, he said it out of mere kindness, but his frank approval meant very much to me, and to Katherine. I had talked so much about F— and of my admiration for him that it would have gone hard with us both if there had been a trace of hesitation to his welcome. But when he, who read little, spoke out his delight in her story, 'The Woman at the Store', our cup of happiness brimmed over. Katherine and F— became fast friends thenceforward. Six years afterwards, F— was the witness to our marriage, and Katherine gave me for a wedding-present one of his pictures, which she saved up to buy.[18]

After this meeting, affectionate mimicry of Fergusson appears in Mansfield's letters; she copies his phrase 'this art business' and imitates the 'Cheer-oh' with which he ends his letters (possibly a written version of a colloquial Scottish pronunciation of 'cheerio'). When she was ill in London he visited her frequently and cheered her up: 'Have you ever heard him refer to a person's state of health as "one foot in the grave and the other on a banana skin". Oh! that does make me laugh so.'[19] She attributes the affinity between them to a quality they share; she writes about it to Murry:

> I feel so immensely conscious of my own roots. You could pull and pull & pull at me–Ill not come out–You could cut off my flowers–others will grow–Now I feel that equally…of you–and *Johnny* has roots.[20]

The functional beauty of his studio indicates another significant link between them which is more than just a question of personal taste. Visitors to Fergusson's studio describe its

> almost scientific cleanliness…on a small white table there was a dark bowl full to the brim, not of flowers, but of those peculiarly

shrill pink matchstalks which were at that time a common object of the Parisian café table. Fergusson evidently liked that colour.[21]

What Ida Baker writes of Mansfield could apply equally to Fergusson; both lived their colourist aesthetic, and created an environment that expressed their obsession with line and design:

> Wherever she was…Katherine made and kept her 'home' as beautiful and expressive as possible. There was no untidiness or any kind of confusion, so that however poor and sparse her possessions, her sense of order and form always imparted a feeling of space and beauty. Of course this was the expression of her inner self, for ever discarding extraneous matter and imposing form and order.
>
> Katherine hated 'fuzzy edges'.[22]

Mansfield's work was transformed by her encounter with the *Rhythm* group, but pleasure in order and form in her domestic life was disrupted by the financial chaos the magazine caused her and Murry. 'The Woman at the Store' appeared in *Rhythm* in the spring of 1912; by the next issue the publisher was no longer the St Catherine Press but Mansfield's publisher, Stephen Swift, and the magazine began to appear monthly rather than quarterly. This happened because Murry overreached himself as editor, failing to understand the financial implications of what he was doing. *Rhythm* began with £50 from Professor Sadler, the father of Michael Sadler, who was initially the co-editor of the magazine with Murry; Frederick Goodyear was also involved as a contributor from the beginning, with Fergusson as a very active art editor. The publishers told Murry that he should have 3000 copies of the magazine printed, but he did not realize the significance of the phrase 'sale or return'. When the large number of unsold copies of the first four issues were returned, he found he was financially responsible just at the moment when he had announced that *Rhythm* would appear monthly. Stephen Swift then became the publisher of the next five[23] (monthly) numbers, paying Murry and Mansfield £10 per month as editors. In the summer of 1912, the patron of the arts Edward Marsh began to take an interest in *Rhythm*, having been introduced to Murry and Mansfield by Rupert Brooke. Thinking that the magazine was becoming more secure, Mansfield and Murry took a cottage in the country near Chichester on a three-year lease, but then Swift went bankrupt, leaving them with a debt of £400. Mansfield's allowance from her father went in monthly instalments to the printers. Martin Secker took on publication, producing the magazine more cheaply; its appearance changed, and it included advertisements for Heal's and for 'The Parma Rooms', a salon for 'scientific hair-brushing' which Ida Baker had opened with a colleague. Murry and Mansfield lived in a one-room flat for a while, hoping to keep *Rhythm* going. Fergusson withdrew as art editor at the point when Secker took over, and the magazine became less avant-garde as a result, reusing drawings by Fergusson and Rice that had already appeared in earlier issues; it folded in 1913. It was revived as the *Blue Review* in May 1913, but after three monthly issues it too failed. Murry was being pursued for *Rhythm*'s debts throughout this time, and he and Mansfield lived at six different addresses between April 1912 and December 1913, some of them extremely cramped and depressing, and one of them verminous. She writes to Murry at this time of her resentment of domestic chores: '[W]hen I have to clean up twice over or wash up extra unnecessary things I get frightfully impatient and want to be working. So often, this week, Ive heard you and Gordon talking while I washed dishes.'[24] Two years later the yearning is more intense, not just for freedom from domestic drudgery but for stability and children: 'Why haven't I got a real "home", a real life…Im not a girl – Im a woman. I *want* things. Shall I ever have them?'[25] She and Murry moved to Paris in December 1913, where Mansfield met Murry's friend Francis Carco who had written for *Rhythm*, but they were forced to return to London in February 1914 so that Murry, a declared bankrupt, could work as the art critic of the *Westminster Gazette*.

Their restless attempts to escape financial pressure put a strain on their relationship and on their literary productivity. D. H. Lawrence and Frieda, who became their friends in 1913, were able to marry in July 1914; Murry and Mansfield were witnesses at the wedding, but were unable to marry themselves because Mansfield was not divorced from Bowden. At the wedding, Frieda gave Mansfield the ring from her first marriage; Mansfield wore it for the rest of her life, and was buried with it. Mansfield and Murry began to meet people connected with Bloomsbury at this time, such as the painter Mark

Gertler; they also became fond of S. S. Koteliansky, who thought Mansfield 'had the greatest talent for being a human being he had ever known'.[26] Murry enlisted at the outbreak of the First World War in August 1914, but was given a medical exemption the next day; Mansfield had an attack of pleurisy in 1914, and her cough worsened. However, domestic and financial anxiety made her long for freedom, and in 1915 she decided that her three-year idyll with Murry was over, and made a risky trip to visit Francis Carco, who was stationed at Gray in France as a military postman. The episode eventually proved more valuable as copy than as a love affair, and she returned to Murry, who knew where and with whom she had been and waited, rightly confident that the affair would prove disappointing to her. Her brother Leslie, who had arrived from New Zealand to join up in February 1915, spent his last leave with Mansfield in the autumn; by then Lawrence and Murry had begun another magazine, *Signature*, which only ran to three issues, and Murry had become the reviewer of French books for the *Times Literary Supplement*. Almost immediately some of their friends and acquaintances became casualties of war: Rupert Brooke died in April 1915 and the sculptor Gaudier-Brzeska in June. Mansfield wrote to her brother in August saying that this 'is not a letter. It is only my arms round you for a quick minute.'[27] Early in October he was killed in a hand-grenade accident in France.

Her brother's death was the catalyst for a change of direction in Mansfield's work which will be discussed in the next chapter, but the change developed out of what she had learnt from her involvement with the Rhythmists, the focus of this chapter. Many of them were artists in a state of voluntary exile, as she was. Anne Estelle Rice and the sculptor Jo Davidson were Americans living in Paris, with other Anglo-American Fauves such as Jessica Dismorr, Ethel Wright and William Zorach; Fergusson's fellow Scot, S. J. Peploe, joined him in Paris. What they all enjoyed about being there was the freedom they experienced from the boundaries imposed by academicians. Mansfield had three phases of living in Paris, sometimes quite briefly, at this time, and she shared vicariously in Murry's more extensive first-hand experience of the artistic and intellectual excitement there. The conservatism of British society by comparison is revealed in the response in 1910 to Fry's exhibition, 'Manet and the Post-Impressionists'. The work of painters that had been familiar

to viewers in Parisian galleries for years caused an outcry: Robert
Ross, writing in the *Morning Post*, saw it apocalyptically as 'a wide-
spread plot to destroy the whole fabric of European painting'.[28]
Desmond McCarthy's introduction to the catalogue for the exhibition explains for a British audience the distinction between
Impressionism and Post-Impressionism, encapsulating in so doing
the dynamic that drove the Rhythmists:

> The Post-Impressionists consider the Impressionists too naturalis-
> tic … Impressionism encouraged an artist to paint a tree as it
> appeared to him at the moment under particular circumstances.
> It insisted so much upon the importance of his rendering his
> exact impression that his work often completely failed to express
> a tree at all; as transferred to canvas it was just so much shimmer
> and colour. The 'treeness' of the tree was not rendered at all; all
> the emotion and associations such as trees may be made to con-
> vey in poetry were omitted.[29]

It was the audience's emotion and instinct that the Rhythmists,
influenced by Bergson, were interested in stimulating in their art.
Anticipating the title of their magazine, McCarthy focuses on an element of savagery in the paintings of Matisse:

> [S]earch for an abstract harmony of line, for rhythm, has been
> carried to lengths which often deprive the figure of all appear-
> ance of nature. The general effect of his pictures is that of a
> return to primitive, even perhaps of a return to barbaric,
> art … [The artist] begins to try to unload, to simplify the drawing
> and painting, by which natural objects are evoked, in order to
> recover the lost expressiveness and life.[30]

The Rhythmists found Paris stimulating because there the return
to the barbaric, with its simplifying of line and its emphasis on
rhythm, was happening in a wide variety of art forms and in philosophy simultaneously. Bergson was writing and lecturing; the first
Fauvist movement of Matisse, Derain and Vlaminck had been continued by Rice, Fergusson and their friends; Diaghilev's Ballets
Russes appeared in Paris for the first time in 1910; music by Debussy
and Stravinsky provided the scores for the Ballets Russes from 1910

until 1913; Isadora Duncan's modern dance company performed in Paris. Fergusson describes it like this:

> It was in these pre-war days that Middleton Murry and Michael Sadler came over and asked me to be the art editor of *Rhythm*. Peploe contributed to it. Later Murry came with Katherine Mansfield. We were all very excited with the Russian Ballet when it came to Paris. Bakst was a *Sociétaire* of the Salon d'Automne and used all the ideas of modern painting for his *décor*. Diaghilev made a triumph, surely even greater than he had hoped for. No wonder S. J. said these were some of the greatest nights of his life. They were the greatest nights in anyone's life – *Sheherazade*, *Petruchka*, *Sacre du Printemps*, Nijinski, Karsavina, Fokine. But we didn't spend all our evenings at the Russian ballet; there was the Cirque Médrano, the Concert-Mayol and the Gaité-Montparnasse.[31]

Their freedom and joy in discovery was evidently partly the result of voluntary exile from their own national, social and familial constraints. Frederick Goodyear's opening essay, 'The New Thelema', in the first issue of *Rhythm*, associates the idea of the exile or outcast with discovery of the deep structures of the self: 'it is neo-barbarians, men and women who to the timid and unimaginative seem merely perverse and atavistic, that must familiarize us with our outcast selves'.[32] The exuberant tone of Fergusson's description of life in Paris in the first years of the twentieth century is carried into the pages of *Rhythm*.

The most immediately striking aspect of the magazine, even after almost a century which has been characterized by developing sophistication in graphic design, is the beauty of its physical appearance. The cover is elephant grey,[33] with a version of Fergusson's large oil painting, also called *Rhythm*, in strongly marked black lines. The emphatic elemental curves of the tree behind the naked female figure are exaggerated by seating the woman on a semi-circle rather than on the drapery of the painting. In both versions the curve of the back is intersected by a brutal vertical line, and in both the woman holds an apple that mirrors the shape of her aggressively jutting breasts. She seems an intimidating Eve; in both versions the face is half shaded and not particularized, and as Antliff suggests, by 'portraying her naked in abstract settings, he removes her from any modern-day or social context and suggests a mythological one'.[34]

The magazine is printed on thick, deckle-edged paper with wide margins, its physical texture conveying to the reader a sensation of presence and vitality; decorative headings and tailpieces as well as drawings and paintings are interspersed throughout the text. Some of the most arresting images are repeated from one issue of the magazine to another, creating a rhythm for the reader, and signalling visually links between articles. For instance, the headpiece of a thoughtful little face appears in the first issue above Sadler's article on 'Fauvism and a Fauve' and recurs in subsequent issues, as do the illuminated capital T of the first issue, the tiger catching a monkey by its tail, and several of Dismorr's angular and expressive human figures. Jessica Dismorr, Anne Estelle Rice, Henri Gaudier-Brzeska and J. D. Fergusson in particular make a strength of the magazine's lack of colour reproduction: for example, Rice's illustrations of *Schéhérazade* for her own article on '*Les Ballets Russes*' in *Rhythm* (vol. II, no. 7, August 1912, pp. 106 and 109) express the theme of the magazine through the strength of its sinuous lines, and the congruity between the dancing female figures and the twirling drapery behind them.

The central way in which *Rhythm* expresses its Bergsonian principles is in its form. It manifestly challenges the homogeneous in favour of heterogeneity; Bergson describes duration as being a succession of changes that melt into each other like the successive notes of a piece of music, not a measurable and definable series of separable entities. The way in which the magazine does this at its best is to explore one art in terms of another, with an emphasis on internationalism, both in the range of its contributors and in the material it covers. Painters depict, crudely and strongly, a response to what they have seen in a dance performance; Jessica Dismorr's *Isadora* juxtaposes an angular and dramatic figure in white against curving black drapery and communicates power rather than what the dancer looked like, in the style of a *Jugendstil* design. Music critics interpret their subject through another art: Rollo Myers writes:

> Debussy's music is often called Impressionist, and rightly; but it is something more: it is in its essence Fauvist. That is to say it does not only aim at securing an impression of things as they are, but it aims at reflecting their psychological effect on the mind of the observer.[35]

Women were empowered within the *Rhythm* group, though my description of the monumental woman on the cover as Eve might seem to contradict this. A viewing of either the painting or the cover elicits contradictory sensations in that the woman is evidently associated with fertility, and yet she is muscular and commanding rather than yielding and passive. Elizabeth Cumming reads her 'as the source of natural life' which 'relates to her in the form of a gently curving tree and its product, fruit. There is a sense of calm, growth and conclusion to the work.'[36] The sharply vertical, truncating line on the right seems to me to preclude a sense of calm; the disturbance it generates may relate to Cumming's claim that 'to Fergusson she was the Bergsonian impulse of life',[37] or *élan vital*. The figure's feet are almost cloven, and certainly look as if she is on tip-toe, poised to move, not sedentary.[38] For the first time in his career, Fergusson was painting female nudes, often using their breasts as the focus for the painting, as for instance in *At my Studio Window* (1910), *Torse de Femme* (1910–11) and *Voiles Indiennes* (1910–11). Antliff explains what I have described as a contradictory response in the viewer to these paintings in this way:

> [D]espite the opposition posed here between female and male principles it should be remembered that both were conjoined in the primal élan vital. Any of the élan vital's gendered manifestations could possess varying amounts of female or male élan, and Fergusson, in his decorative works, conflated the signs of male and female sexuality in an attempt to grasp durée [Bergson's duration] at its pansexual origin.[39]

The complexity of gender identity, its heterogeneity rather than homogeneity, that is explored in *Rhythm* became one of the preoccupations of Mansfield's fiction, for instance in 'Psychology', 'At the Bay' and 'The Daughters of the Late Colonel'. In *Rhythm*, many of the drawings are of naked female figures, often holding baskets of fruit and dancing with other women. They are not, however, passive or coy objects of a male gaze; they are empowered and vigorous, evocative of the throbbing rhythm of Stravinsky's *Sacre du Printemps*, rather than western versions of seductive tunes from the harem. They embody the ideology of *Rhythm* and its contributors:

> [T]he *Rhythm* critics could assert that a female artist was in posses-
> sion of a male gendered artistic 'will to power', a claim they in fact
> made for Anne Estelle Rice. Thus the binary opposition between
> male and female élan could dissipate, and gender categories
> become unstable, depending on the ideological import of the art or
> art criticism. Any conception of artistic creativity as an end in itself,
> or of male artists as the 'origin' of such creative forces is likewise
> negated. In Bergson's monistic theory of creative evolution, the
> élan vital transcends its gendered manifestations, both male and
> female.[40]

Just as *Rhythm* expresses in its physical appearance its contributors'
will to transcend conventional boundaries between the arts, its fluid
movement between drawings and text embodies its rejection of conventional gender, social and academic identities.

The young editor, Murry, wanted *Rhythm* to be the cosmopolitan
organ of modernism. Because he and Fergusson never attempted to
define what they meant by rhythm, its nebulous quality was initially a strength in that it allowed all the contributors to take off
with their own ideas of what they were doing, and eventually a
weakness in that it could not be sustained, though it made the radical statement of heterogeneity that was its prime objective. Its creative writing is generally lacklustre and deficient in the ' "guts" and
bloodiness'[41] that Murry was aiming at in comparison with the
essays and artwork. While the female breast becomes a potent visual
image in the magazine's illustrations, it has a weary Orientalist
familiarity in W. L. George's poem, 'The Negress': 'Oh, maid with
breasts as black as ebony, / Say, are for me the languors of your
eyes?'[42] The awkward juxtaposition of breasts and eyes becomes
both clichéd and comic in Murry's own poem, 'Life', in the same
issue: 'She is fair / Her breasts like towers, and her chestnut hair /
Flowing and fragrant, and her dancing eyes / Will burst with passion.'[43] The revolutionary bloodiness that Murry aspired to in the
magazine is inadequately represented by his picture of exploding
eyes surmounting architectural breasts. The intellectual distinction
of *Rhythm* is most evident in its essays, though not those written
jointly by Murry and Mansfield, where Bergson's philosophy is
expressed as a kind of snobbery: 'Intuition is a purely aristocratic

quality. It is the power of divining individuality in other persons and other things.'[44] Murry's condescending self-righteousness is often irksome; in a ludicrous essay he likens Frank Harris to Shakespeare, and attempts rhetorically to identify himself with the rejected genius: 'The soul of England is dead. It justifies itself by stoning the prophets, year after year stoning the prophets.'[45]

Frederick Goodyear expresses a comparable idea with much greater trenchancy, and insight into the *Zeitgeist*, in 'The New Thelema'. The title is taken from Rabelais' Abbey of Thélème, whose founder's law is 'Do what thou wilt', an edict based on the belief that men who are genuinely free have a natural instinct prompting them to virtuous action. Like Murry, Goodyear is concerned with radical art, but he engages with the impetus that drives the artist, instead of whining about the public's reception of the new art:

> [T]he pioneers are often scorned and buffeted during their life-time, because they seem deliberately to have forsaken civilization and sought to rebarbarise themselves. This is far from the truth. The call of the wild greensickness, *nostalgie de la boue* – name it how you will – is a true impulse towards conscious freedom. It comes to men who see instinctively that no man is certainly free till all men are free.[46]

This aesthetic combines aspects of Mansfield's experience and aspiration. A woman 'with the taint of the pioneer in my blood', she always responded to the idea of exploration in art and life; she and Murry, in a joint essay for *Rhythm*, declare that, in art, true 'seriousness is an assertion, a courageous acceptance of the unexplored'.[47] She was much closer to the source of Goodyear's metaphor than her British colleagues in that she had seen an exported British form of civilization imposing itself on a wild landscape and on an existing and ancient oral culture; her resentment of the restraints on her own freedom that resulted from that encounter and her contempt for bourgeois Wellington's determined respectability, were compounded by what she saw of the Maoris' entrapment. Now, instead of playing at being a wild cat and making love like a wild beast, as she had done in her entry in Orton's journal, she could reconcile her personal behaviour with her artistic impetus. Her new nickname, Tiger, abbreviated by Murry to 'Tig', remained with her for the rest of her life and signalled the beginning of that paring down process, the simplifying of line to reveal the essentials without stating them, the use of colour to communicate mood and tone, that were characteristic of Fauvism and of her mature fiction. She wrote to Murry, when he asked her to alter a story for the *Blue Review*:

> Im a powerful stickler for form … I hate the sort of licence that English people give themselves – – to spread over and flop and roll about. I feel as fastidious as though I wrote with acid.[48]

The essays in *Rhythm* are part of the reader's experience of rhythmic form, investigating the themes of barbarism and its relationship with deep structures, roots, recurrently, from a variety of perspectives. Murry states the magazine's aims and ideals in the first issue, using an unacknowledged quotation from the Irish dramatist J. M. Synge:

> 'Before art can be human it must learn to be brutal.' Our intention is to provide art, be it drawing, literature or criticism, which shall be vigorous, determined, which shall have its roots below the surface, and be the rhythmical echo of the life with which it is in touch. Both in its pity and its brutality it shall be real.[49]

In the next issue, Sadler's essay 'The Letters of Vincent Van Gogh' shows how the Fauvists grew out of Van Gogh's experiments, quoting his tentative definitions of himself in relation to the Impressionists. His use of colour was very different from theirs: 'Colour so filled his mind, that he got to see moods expressed by different colours and combinations of colour.'[50] He was much less confident than Gauguin about what he was doing, and about making distinctions between his own work and the Impressionists' paintings; Sadler quotes a letter in which he says: 'I am only now beginning to try a simplified technique, which could not perhaps be called "impressionist".'[51] In his summarizing comparison of the Impressionists, whom he defines as realists, and Van Gogh who is teaching himself to be brutal in his use of paint, Sadler reiterates one of *Rhythm*'s thematic preoccupations: an exploration of the boundaries between Impressionism and Post-Impressionism, and between the Aesthetic Movement and Modernism:

> The neo-impressionists used their technique to give an effect of light; they were realists. Vincent strove for brilliance of colour as

a means to design and, as has been seen, to suggest deeper meaning…'I follow no system in painting; I flog the canvas with
irregular strokes and let them stand. Impasto – here and there
uncovered patches – overpainting – brutalities…No photographic imitation, that is the chief thing'.[52]

In the next issue of *Rhythm* Sadler pursues the theme of discovering barbarism in an essay on Gauguin called '*L'Esprit Veille*'. Gauguin
did not take civilization to Tahiti, but discovered himself and his
style through what Sadler describes as savagery: ' "Your civilization is
your disease," he wrote to Strindberg, "my barbarism is my restoration to health." '[53] In a brilliantly written and vigorously illustrated
essay by Anne Estelle Rice these ideas about civilization, barbarism
and deep structures are explored in relation to an innovative art of
the moment, not of the recent past. In 1910 Sergei Diaghilev broke
away from the repressive and bureaucratic regime of the Imperial
Theatres in Russia and by the next year the Ballets Russes had
become a company. He had already organized a major exhibition of
Russian art at the Salon d'Automne in 1906; when such artists as
Vaslav Nijinsky left the Maryinsky and Bolshoi companies to join
him, he was able to put on a series of new ballets which helped
to mould the ideology of the *Rhythm* group. The first night of
Schéhérazade in 1910 was revolutionary:

> Nothing like it had ever been seen before. It was not just the
> dancing of Rubinstein as Zobéide, Nijinsky as the Golden Negro
> and Alexis Bulgarov as the Shah that was astounding, it was the
> whole production – music, décor, costumes, lighting – all com-
> bined into forty minutes of pure and overwhelming sensation,
> that made it so memorable.[54]

The Firebird, with music by Stravinsky, was also performed in 1910;
in 1912, a sensation was caused by the first performance of *L'Après-
midi d'un faune*. Its impact must have resonated with the *Rhythm*
group because it was so overt in its rejection of traditional balletic
conventions and romantic music, and in its return to an emphasis
on classical line and poses. Rice's essay includes a drawing of the
frieze-like postures of the nymphs and the faun. The languorous
piece opens with the faun playing his pipe; seven nymphs join him,
and one tantalizes him by shedding her outer veils and revealing

herself in a brief golden tunic. He is left, on their departure, only with one of the veils. He nuzzles it, lowers himself on to it, and reaches stylized orgasm with a convulsive jerk in the final moment. The faun is a pagan creature, and the music is disorientating

> for as the music goes on we hear an exotic strain; and it seems that this must come from Cyprus, or from Crete with its dark pleasures, or from Daphne, the grove of love near Antioch, or from Thessaly, through which the train of Bacchus had to pass, bringing the dangerous gift of wine from Asia.[55]

This description, by a ballet critic rather than a painter, substantiates Rollo Myers' claim that Debussy's music is Fauvist.

Anne Estelle Rice's essay, '*Les Ballets Russes*', with its illustrations which emphasize line, addresses the impact of the *élan vital* of the ballets on their audience:

> The Russian ballets are elemental to the last degree, full of the visions of Asia, a tropical heat, not of stillness, but of new life born every instant, where realism and fantasy combine and multiply into a fluidity of moving reds, blues, oranges, greens, purples, triangles, squares, circles, serpentine and zigzag shapes.[56]

Her main focus is on the contribution of Léon Bakst, who was like Fergusson a *sociétaire* of the Salon d'Automne, and whose work shows parallels with the Fauves. He designed the costumes and sets for, among other ballets, *Schéhérazade*, *L'Après-midi d'un faune* and *Daphnis and Chloë*. Rice's emphasis in her essay is on the Fauvism of his costumes and sets, with its dynamic use of colour:

> Bakst takes all colours, every nuance of each colour from its extreme brilliancy downwards, and all directions of line and compositions of line, harmonizes everything; and by his simple but fully expressive effect, convinces the spectator of the artist's belief in his power to create, as opposed to the apologetic grovelling of the aesthetic before nature.[57]

Her claim is that the artist can rival nature in his or her creativity. Rice became one of Mansfield's closest friends; it is easy to see why Mansfield was attracted to her. The vitality and commitment of

Rice's writing combined with her astute powers of observation are all evident in her summary of Bakst's creativity:

> A painter in line, a painter in movement, a painter in forms, he knows the value of line to give energy and force, the value of a dominant colour and shape, the value of daring juxtapositions to create life and movement in masses of colour, where costumes, drapery and decorations reverberate to sound, action, and light. The modern tendency in all forms of art is towards 'la recherche des lignes,' which in their quality and direction must be 'les lignes vivantes,' or the result is banal and sterile. The genial and dominant idea of the Russian Ballets is based upon *line*.[58]

One of the appealing aspects of *Rhythm* once Mansfield had joined its editorial team was that it did not take itself too seriously, in spite of its impassioned commitment to Fauvism. Though its controlling dictum, 'Before art can be human it must learn to be brutal', was taken from Synge, the Two Tigers wrote a piece for the seventh issue of *Rhythm* entitled 'Jack and Jill attend the theatre' which is a parody of *The Well of the Saints*. It takes the form of a dialogue between Jack and Jill who are present at a performance of the play; Murry was generally known as 'Jack':

> *Jill*   Eh! Glory be to God and here we are, Jack. And isn't it a grand thing for a woman to be sitting on a velvet seat, and she with her man beside her in a boiled shirt and all.
> *Jack*   Whist! woman, when I tell ye – they'll be after pulling up the curtain, and it's myself will be destroyed entirely.[59]

Given Mansfield's ability to mimic and wear other writers' literary clothes, the reader can guess which of the Two Tigers wrote 'Sunday Lunch' by 'The Tiger'. It concerns a lunch party, 'Sunday lunch is the last of the cannibal feasts', for the smart literary and artistic set in London, possibly with a Bloomsbury tinge; here the hostess is trying to make her guests mingle, though who is introducing whom to whom becomes tangled:

> Takes the guest's arm. 'Now I want to introduce you to Kaila Scarrotski. He's Hungarian. And he's been doing those naked backs for that café. And I know you know all about Hungary, and

those extraordinary places. He's just read your "Pallors of Passion" and he swears you've Slav blood.' She presses the guest's hand thereby conveying: 'Prove that you have. Remember I didn't ask you to my lunch to wait until the food was served and then eat it and go. Beat your tom-tom, dear.'[60]

The cultural icons of the period and of Fauvism, which Mansfield used herself, are mocked when the host of the party meets his guest: ' "Glad you came." Takes guest aside. "I say, that French dancing woman's here. Over there – on the leopard skin – with the Chinese fan. Pitch into her, there's a good chap." '[61]

The *Blue Review*, which took over from *Rhythm*, in no way replaced it; the new magazine is much more conventional and compartmentalized than *Rhythm* and lacks its visual impact. It is remarkable only because it signals the encounter between D. H. Lawrence and Murry; Lawrence thought *Rhythm* itself 'a daft paper, but the folk seem rather nice'.[62] As a result he gave them a story, 'The Soiled Rose', for nothing. It appeared in the *Blue Review* as *Rhythm* was defunct by then. Both the story and a review of current German fiction which Lawrence wrote for Murry suggest that he might have had some sympathy for the ideology that galvanized the writers and artists involved with *Rhythm*. In his review of Thomas Mann's *Death in Venice* he writes:

[E]ven while he has a rhythm in style, yet his work has none of the rhythm of a living thing, the rise of a poppy, then the after uplift of the bud, the shedding of the calyx and the spreading wide of the petals, the falling of the flower and the pride of the seed-head.[63]

The story's title 'The Soiled Rose' is ironic in that Hilda, the rose, seems to gain from her experience of loving first of all a young intellectual, Syson, and then the local gamekeeper, rather than being damaged by it, though from Syson's perspective she has aged and matured rather startlingly. The story, like *Lady Chatterley's Lover*, has what could be described as Colourist as well as Fauvist elements with its stabs of colour, as when Hilda takes the visitor into the keeper's secret lair:

On the floor were patchwork rugs of cat-skin, and a red calf-skin, while hanging from the wall were other furs. Hilda took down one, which she put on. It was a cloak of rabbit-skin edged with white fur, and with a hood, apparently of the skins of stoats. She laughed at Syson from out of this barbaric mantle.[64]

Hilda's deliberate identification with barbarism is a choice that she is able to make. In three of the stories she wrote for *Rhythm* and the *Blue Review* Mansfield explores the savagery of a group of pakeha New Zealanders who have much more limited choices. Later she would not allow these stories to be collected; while they lack the subtlety and indirection of '*Je ne parle pas français*' they are impressive for their Fauvist vigour and have a Bergsonian dimension in their portrayal of the self. 'The Woman at the Store' and 'Ole Underwood', which was dedicated to Anne Estelle Rice, were published in *Rhythm*, in Spring 1912 and January 1913 respectively, and 'Millie' appeared in the *Blue Review* in June 1913. Questions about gender identity link the three stories; 'The Woman at the Store' and 'Millie' are set in the backblocks of New Zealand and 'Ole Underwood' takes place in Wellington. The three protagonists are all in a kind of limbo, both social and psychological. The woman has been neglected by her husband, and left to run the store and endure miscarriages while he goes off shearing; Millie has no role and no children so she sits about 'thinking of nothing at all'.[65] Ole Underwood has been in prison for 20 years for murdering his wife; though he is now technically free, his past is known to the community and he is regarded as 'cracked'. In all the stories the participants' savagery partly takes the form of an inability to articulate their feelings, which leads each of the three to violence. The woman tells her hearers of weeks of isolation with her sickly child:

> 'Oh, some days – an' months of them – I 'ear them two words knockin' inside me all the time – "Wot for!" but sometimes I'll be cooking the spuds an' I lifts the lid off to give 'em a prong and I 'ears, quite suddin again, "Wot for!" '

(558)

Millie 'didn't know what was the matter with herself that afternoon. She could have a good cry – just for nothing – and then change her blouse and have a good cup of tea' (572). Ole Underwood walks about shouting 'Ah-k!' All three are gendered in ways that seem to confuse them, and all three stories are Fauvist in the manner of Van

Gogh's paintings. They are unremittingly intense, characterized by abrupt and terse sentences rather like violent impasto; their colour is heightened and their rhythm is insistent.

The distorted vision in 'The Woman at the Store' is clear in that the narrator is dazed by heat and falling asleep in a surreal setting:

> There is no twilight in our New Zealand days, but a curious half-hour when everything appears grotesque – it frightens – as though the savage spirit of the country walked abroad and sneered at what it saw.
>
> (554)

Everyone in the story seems touched by the savage and grotesque, and relationships are muddied in a way that implicates the reader. In the *Rhythm* version of the story which is likely to be more authentic, 'Jim' appears throughout as 'Hin', which sounds like a Maori name, but his racial identity is never clarified. When Jo is creeping towards a nocturnal encounter with the woman, the narrator says: 'alas! my poor brother!' (561) but there is no other allusion to the relationship. The assumption is likely to be that the narrator is male because the group who arrive at the store seem to have the camaraderie of fellow workmen, but the sinister 'kid' reveals that she has been spying on the narrator who has been seen 'with no clothes on in the creek. I looked at her where she couldn't see me from' (557). Just as the narrator's gender identity is confusing, so is the woman's. Hin promises Jo a woman 'with blue eyes and yellow hair' (551) but when they meet her she is more of a puppet than an object of sexual desire:

> Certainly her eyes were blue, and what hair she had was yellow, but ugly. She was a figure of fun. Looking at her, you felt there was nothing but sticks and wires under that pinafore – her front teeth were knocked out, she had red, pulpy hands.
>
> (552–3)

Yet Hin remembers her as being 'pretty as a wax doll' (556), a sinister image in that she has been melted down into something repulsive. The narrator's initial picture of her is accurate, in that she has had to be both male and female; she seems to be carrying a black stick, but this is because the narrator does not associate women with rifles. The woman's very sexuality, the fact that she once knew a hundred and twenty-five different ways of kissing, has destroyed her gender identity as her husband has repeatedly reappeared, made her pregnant, and then left her:

> 'It's six years since I was married, and four miscarriages. I says to 'im, I says, what do you think I'm doin' up 'ere? If you was back at the Coast I'd 'ave you lynched for child murder.'
>
> (558)

Gender categories here are unstable not because binary oppositions are being contested and undermined, as they were by *Rhythm*'s artists, but because an exhausted woman has to play the female role of bearing children, and the traditionally male one of defending herself and her children against violence, by shooting her husband. Her store has run out of supplies as her body failed to feed her child: 'I 'adn't any milk till a month after she was born' (555).

Just as the mother has become a brute, the child is preternaturally aged by her situation. As C. K. Stead suggests, the reader is likely to misread the implication of the mother's repeated threats to prevent the child revealing her secrets in her drawings: 'Subtly the story has led us to expect something pornographic.'[66] The child's terrible secret drives her to a state of almost erotic near-hysteria like her mother's: 'she worked herself up into a mad excitement, laughing and trembling, and shooting out her arms' (559). In this last gesture she is enacting her secret, which is the knowledge that her mother has killed her father. The fact that she draws 'extraordinary and repulsively vulgar' pictures implies that she, like her mother, cannot do more than gesture towards communication with other human beings. Both are trapped in a limbo world, a store with no customers and no stock. Any sense of cultural identity seems to be parodic, a bitter reflection from the elemental backwoods on the expectations of the 'parent' culture: 'It was a large room, the walls plastered with old pages of English periodicals. Queen Victoria's Jubilee appeared to be the most recent number. A table with an ironing board and wash-tub on it' (553). The fact that the woman has been ironing seems to prove her insanity: 'Imagine bothering about ironing. *Mad*, of course she's mad!' (554). The revelation of past violence hints at violence to come, as Jo waves his companions off and shouts that he will pick them up later: 'A bend in the road, and the whole place disappeared' (562). The comment about the narrator's poor brother now seems prophetic; the place seems to have been a nightmare vision which has gone, taking him with it in the same way that the husband disappeared.

The setting of 'Millie' is as savage as that of 'The Woman at the Store'. The perspective throughout is Millie's, and she is suffering from visual distortion which reflects her confusion about colonial identity and gender:

> In the distance along the dusty road she could see the horses, like brown spots dancing up and down, and when she looked away from them and over the burnt paddocks she could see them still – just before her eyes, jumping like mosquitoes. It was half-past two in the afternoon. The sun hung in the faded blue sky like a burning mirror, and away beyond the paddocks the blue mountains quivered and leapt like the sea.
>
> (571)

Size is inverted with horses as mosquitoes, the elements are transposed as earth becomes water; the heat skews Millie's vision so that the reader sees the world through her lenses, and it is heightened and distorted like a painting by Van Gogh or Munch. She looks at 'the suggestively-named Willie Cox'[67] and thinks he is 'a bit too free and easy for her taste' (571). As in 'The Woman at the Store', two pictures on the walls of the house encapsulate the gender identity her society prescribes. One is English:

> She flopped down on the side of the bed and stared at the coloured print on the wall opposite, *Garden Party at Windsor Castle*. In the foreground emerald lawns planted with immense oak trees, and in their grateful shade a muddle of ladies and gentlemen and parasols and little tables. The background was filled with the towers of Windsor Castle, flying three Union Jacks, and in the middle of the picture the old Queen, like a tea-cosy with a head on top of it.
>
> (572)

The scene is full of icons of the old country, rather comically conflated when the Queen appears as a tea-cosy, but oaks, lawns and towers are linked with the flag of empire to define national identity. Millie rejects it as having 'Too much side' (573), but her alternative is just as carefully constructed. She looks at her wedding photograph, clearly taken in a studio prepared for the purpose: 'Nice picture that – if you *do* like ... And behind them there were some fern trees and a waterfall, and Mount Cook in the distance, covered with snow' (573). The markers of New Zealand identity as background for the studio portrait have no more substantial link with Millie's present situation than Windsor Castle; the colonial subject is in limbo between the two constructions of nationality. This is reflected in the narrative, in that a local sheep farmer has been killed and there is a general assumption about who the culprit is, based on no evidence at all:

> Willie Cox said they found him in the barn, shot bang through the head, and the young English 'johnny' who'd been on the station learning farming – disappeared. Funny! she couldn't think of anyone shooting Mr. Williamson, and him so popular and all. My word! when they caught that young man! Well, you couldn't be sorry for a young fellow like that. As Sid said, if he wasn't strung up where would they all be? A man like that doesn't stop at one go.
>
> (572)

A sequence of suppositions based on xenophobic prejudices shifts the young man from apprentice to serial killer within six short sentences. Sexual and colonial anxiety are repressed presences in the story: 'I wunner why we never had no kids ... ' (573). When Millie discovers that the young supposed culprit is hiding behind her wood stack, gender roles are reversed: ' "I'll teach you to play tricks with a woman," she yelled, and she took a gun' (574). What she discovers is that the supposed murderer has fainted, also reversing gender stereotypes, and this introduces the first moment of deep feeling she has experienced:

> A strange dreadful feeling gripped Millie Evans' bosom – some seed that had never flourished there, unfolded and struck deep roots and burst into painful leaf.
>
> (574)

The powerful metaphor implies that, whatever she tells herself, she is capable of deep maternal feeling; though the 'pain in her bosom half suffocated her' (574) she comforts the boy, who speaks 'in the little voice of a child talking in his sleep' (575). Significantly, the final scene takes place at night; she and Sid are in bed and his muttered 'Good night, ole girl' (576), while hunching the quilt round his shoulders, suggests that what marital ardour he may have had has long since dwindled. Millie asserts to herself that the experience of being moved by the boy's plight has taught her what to think: ' 'E must get off. 'E must. I don't care anythink about justice an' all the rot they've been spoutin' to-night … 'Ow are yer to know what anythink's like till yer *do* know' (576). This confident rejection of patriarchal wisdom is reversed again, in a quasi-sexual scene in which Millie, with 'her night-dress flicking her legs', suddenly roars encouragement to the pursuers, with the heat of the opening scene now transferred to the pursuit. It seems to be Millie's substitute for sexual fulfilment:

> At the sight of Harrison in the distance, and the three men hot after, a strange mad joy smothered everything else. She rushed into the road – she laughed and shrieked and danced in the dust, jigging the lantern. 'A – ah! Arter 'im, Sid! A-a-a-h! Ketch him, Willie. Go it! Go it! A-ah, Sid! Shoot 'im down. Shoot 'im!'
>
> (577)

In both 'The Woman at the Store' and 'Millie' the reader is given an experience of Bergson's duration, that 'succession of qualitative changes, which melt into and permeate one another, without precise outlines'.[68] Mansfield had read *Rhythm* though she had not met Murry and heard the Rhythmists' discussions about Bergson and art when she wrote 'The Woman at the Store'. She was to perfect the inscription of changes in consciousness which melt into one another in subsequent stories, but the surreal and distorted landscape, and the store itself, are a mismatch with the haunting suggested presence of another landscape, so that the reader is provoked into making a comparison that is never overtly articulated, and one blurs into another. It is sunset but there is no twilight; larks in the slate-coloured sky sound like 'slate pencils scraping over its surface' (550); 'wherever we looked there were advertisements for "Camp

Coffee"' (561), meaning that they were surrounded by Camp Coffee's trade mark, an image of empire from India, with a turbaned sepoy serving coffee for his officer. The officer wears the military uniform of a Highland regiment, with a kilt, a plaid and white puttees; the pennant on the tent behind them bears the legend 'READY AYE READY'. The setting hints at the disjunctions of colonialism, where the colonized country has a suppressed consciousness of what is absent or wrong, modelled on the imperial centre: larks should sing with full-throated ease, twilight ought to linger, men are supposed to be in control of their environment. The series of gender stereotypes which do not match the reality are similarly experienced both by characters and readers in 'The Woman at the Store' and 'Millie' as mismatches, and the violence that erupts in both stories could be seen to stem from expectations about gender that are frustrated by the colonial situation.

'Ole Underwood', dedicated to Anne Estelle Rice, is also characterized by violence which is expressed through the rhythm of the story. It is established by the inversion of the usual word-order in the first sentence: 'Down the windy hill stalked Ole Underwood' (562). The largely monosyllabic, emphatic quality of the first paragraph suggests Ole Underwood's impatience and angry fear; the beating of his heart trapped in his chest indicates his frustration at having been a prisoner for 20 years:

> One, two – one, two – never stopping, never changing. He couldn't do anything. It wasn't loud. No, it didn't make a noise – only a thud. One, two – one, two – like someone beating on an iron in prison, someone in a secret place – bang – bang – bang – trying to get free.
>
> (562–3)

Like a refrain throughout the story a pattern of monosyllabic repetitions enacts the beating of Ole Underwood's heart: 'Stop! Stop! Stop! Stop!' (563); 'Red – red – red – red!' (564); 'Kit! Kit! Kit!' (565); 'I will! I will! I will!' (565); 'Mine! Mine! Mine!' (566). The stuttering energy of the prose enacts the protagonist's state of mind and a rhythmical use of colour imitates what Fergusson and Rice were attempting in their paintings. Ole Underwood is depicted through vividly contrasting colours, and red, a dominant colour in the Fauvist palette, is associated with him from the beginning of the story:

> He carried a black umbrella in one hand, in the other a red and white spotted handkerchief knotted into a lump. He wore a black peaked cap like a pilot; gold rings gleamed in his ears and his little eyes snapped like two sparks.
>
> (562)

The story is full of strident colour; the prison is red, there is a 'green mat of grass' (563) in front of the houses that Underwood passes, with yellow hens lurking under a verandah. Underwood's murderous impulses are conveyed indirectly when he crushes the red-haired barmaid's red flowers; he moves through a world of primary colours to stare at some Chinamen, 'their faces yellow as lemons' (565). As the red filter on the story becomes more intense the climax is reached: Underwood boards a ship apparently believing it is his, and glances back 'at the prison perched like a red bird, at the black webby clouds trailing' (566). Though Underwood is not the narrator, the abrupt, terse vocabulary, the repeated possessive pronouns and the thumping repetition, with its emphasis on blood-colour, convey his mental state:

> He grinned, and rolled in his walk, carrying high in his hand the red and white handkerchief. His ship! Mine! Mine! Mine! beat the hammer…He peered in. A man lay sleeping on a bunk – his bunk – a great big man in a seaman's coat with a long fair beard and hair on the red pillow. And looking down upon him from the wall there shone her picture – his woman's picture – smiling and smiling at the big sleeping man.
>
> (566)

His attempt to get out, and escape the relentless beat of his heart, is frustrated by his belief in a stereotype of masculinity that privileges ownership and power; he kills a kitten that has fleetingly elicited a tender response from him.

These three New Zealand stories pivot on an obvious barbarism: each describes one murder and gestures towards a second. In all of them the interest is not primarily in the plot, but in the repression and inarticulacy of the inhabitants of a surreal and brutal landscape.

The simplification of the narrative line in order to suggest a deep structure, of colonial and sexual anxiety, would be radically developed in Mansfield's next New Zealand stories, but the impact on her imagination of Fergusson and the *Rhythm* group was something that she continued to acknowledge. In a letter to Fergusson in 1918 she writes:

> Are you working? You know quite well what I thought of those pictures, don't you. I knew in a way that they would be *like that* but that did not make them any less of a revelation. They are unforgettable.[69]

5
Mansfield and Modernism: November 1915 – December 1918

> I cant imagine how after the war these men can pick up the
> old threads as tho' it had never been. Speaking to *you* Id say
> we have died and live again.[1]

The exuberant modernism of the Russian Ballet, of the Post-
Impressionist exhibitions in London, and specifically of the Fauvist
aesthetic that united Fergusson, Rice, Murry and Mansfield, was put
into a different perspective by the prolonged brutality of the First
World War. What was expected to be a brief skirmish dragged on for
four years; by the end, Mansfield's personal writing is imbued with
it. The repressed horror of her private losing battle with the disease
that was diagnosed in 1917 as tuberculosis emerges in her descriptions of her response to the war. She writes to Murry from France
that the war obsesses her, though 'it' could as easily refer to the disease: 'Its never out of my mind & everything is poisoned by it. Its
here in me the whole time, eating me away – and I am simply terrified by it.'[2] The gradual erosion of her lungs, or 'wings' as she called
them, by the insidious illness is reported to Murry in military terms,
sometimes with gallant cheerfulness: her doctor 'made a tour of the
battlefield. There is no sign of an *advance* by the enemy – they are
still more or less there in force on our left wing'.[3] The stasis which
was illusory in Mansfield's disease was a dominant actual feature of
the war for which the combatants were unprepared:

> The thicker the trench system grew, the less likelihood was
> there of its course being altered even by the weightiest of offen-
> sive effort. The chief effect of two years of bombardment and

trench-to-trench fighting across no man's land was to have created a zone of devastation of immense length, more than 400 miles between the North Sea and Switzerland, but of narrow depth.[4]

The bizarre effect of this is shown in paintings by war artists; at first glance, one of the Australian painter Arthur Streeton's canvases looks like a traditional landscape,[5] with a slow river and trees in the foreground, but a horizontal strip at the top of the picture depicts occupied mud and shell-bursts merging with clouds. As the painting shows, the 'transition from normality to the place of death was abrupt, all the more so because prosperity reigned in the "rear area"; the armies had brought money, and shops, cafés and restaurants flourished'.[6]

Mansfield saw this disconcerting juxtaposition at first hand when, in relatively good health, she went to visit Francis Carco at the front in 1915. She describes how they walked to a restaurant to dinner and saw the wounded coming down the hill, one man looking 'as though he had 2 red carnations over his ears'; with apparent indifference to the sight, they 'ordered sausages & cotelettes and fried potatoes'.[7] As the war continued she had her own equivalent of the red carnations; she wrote to Murry, using a colour from Fergusson's palette, that her handkerchiefs 'look as though I were in the pork butcher trade', and then that 'the crimson lake is back in the paint box'.[8] In a letter to Fergusson she observes yearningly that 'it is a bad thing during this war to be apart from the one or two people who do count in one's life'.[9] She sees her repeated enforced separation from the people she loves, Murry in particular, as deprivation of the only nourishment that can counter the disease that is aptly named consumption. She cannot eat to defeat it; its consumption is more effective than hers. The other remedy that she rejected at this time, as on subsequent occasions, was retreat to a sanatorium:

> I have discovered the ONLY TREATMENT for consumption It is NOT to cut the malade off from life: neither in a sanatorium nor in a land with milk rivers, butter mountains and cream valleys.[10]

There is a pervasive fear of consumption in all its forms in her letters and notebooks by the end of the war. Her own weight dwindled as the war progressed, and she was forced to try to eat in order to prevent herself from being eaten by bacilli. She tries to believe that the end of the war, national consumption of the enemy, will improve her own health:

> Oh Brett – let there be no more War. I have been spending all my days gradually fitting into a smaller & smaller hole as my puff gets less. Now Im in bed – & here I must stay for a bit. This is very cursed: in fact its HELL but I shall get out of it & once we have lain down our knife & fork & agreed to eat no more German Ill be well again.[11]

The smaller and smaller hole suggests being interred rather than being in bed; Hamlet's phrase 'Not where he eats, but where 'a is eaten'[12] haunts Mansfield's personal writing at this period. When the Peace Treaty is signed, her response indicates how far she is from recovering her health through it; she tells Ottoline Morrell she has a food complex. Festivities are to be held in workhouses and she cannot bear to 'think of all these toothless old jaws guzzling for the day – and then of all that beautiful youth feeding the fields of France'.[13] Her brother was one of them.

The expression of a major shift in her attitude to the war, from excited curiosity to an almost anorexic fear of eating as cannibalism, pivots on a poem she wrote about her brother's death early in 1916. In it she dreams of him for the first time since his death; they are at home in New Zealand and she warns him against gathering the poisonous berries which they call 'Dead Man's Bread'. When she wakes she looks for direction:

> By the remembered stream my brother stands
> Waiting for me with berries in his hands...
> 'These are my body. Sister, take and eat.'[14]

The poison has become a kind of sacrament; in consuming the body of her Christ-like brother she will share his fate. There was eventually a macabre consonance between their deaths. The account that she had of her brother's death from his friend told her: 'he said over and over – "God forgive me for all I have done" and just before he died he said "Lift my head, Katy I can't breathe –".'[15] From about this date there are recurrent references to her cough; in 1923, Mansfield had a pulmonary haemorrhage and died because she could not breathe. Though the war did not cause her illness, her grief for her brother quickened its pace; her essential journeys through France in search of a warm climate involved her in strenuous travel, and in being marooned in Paris during a bombardment, both of which worsened her condition.

In 1920, she wrote to her husband, an Oxford graduate, with bitter irony: 'Not being an intellectual I always seem to have to learn things at the risk of my life.'[16] This is evident during the last years of the war. Her experience of disease and of war, and particularly her response to her brother's death, accelerated her professional development as a writer. She tells Murry in 1918, when she is staying in Cornwall near Anne Estelle Rice, now married to the critic Raymond Drey, that 'shes still at the *Blood & Guts* idea – & how far away are we'.[17] Though the pared-down Fauvist aesthetic remains, her thematic and narrative concerns have shifted definitively from the closure of 'The Woman at the Store': 'the plots of my stories leave me perfectly cold'.[18] In *Women's Fiction and the Great War,* Con Coroneos sees Murry's editorial statement in *Rhythm* that art is real in its brutality and pity as anticipating what was required of art, in and immediately after the Great War:

> Disgust, disclosure of the real, the principle of aversion, the valorizing of pity, brutality, and the unsavouriness of truth: these ideals of *Rhythm* constitute the ironic indifferentiation of twentieth-century representations of war. It is an aesthetic which *already* contains the war.[19]

This chapter is concerned with Mansfield's wartime development as a modernist constantly engaged in aesthetic revision in her writing, and her interest in the work and in some cases involvement in the lives of her literary contemporaries: D. H. Lawrence, Virginia Woolf, Joseph Conrad, James Joyce, T. S. Eliot.

Within a month of her brother's death, Mansfield met in London the painter who became one of her closest friends, the Honorable Dorothy Brett, and, through her, she first made the personal acquaintance of some members of the Bloomsbury Group including Mark Gertler, Clive Bell and Lytton Strachey, though these relationships did not develop immediately. Mansfield's mourning for her brother was so intense that she wanted to escape London and find a peaceful place to express her nostalgia in writing. One way of reading

'Dead Man's Bread' is to see the sacramental but poisonous berries as regenerative food for writing, poisoned because it is inextricable from grief.[20] Mansfield writes to Leslie in her diary as if he were the incestuous lover hinted at in 'His Sister's Keeper', but also the poisonous sacrament of the dream: 'You know I can never be Jack's lover again. You have me, you're in my flesh as well as in my soul.'[21] Murry and she went to Bandol in the South of France, and, in unpromising circumstances, began the happiest phase of their life together, at the Villa Pauline. On 16 February 1916 Mansfield wrote to her dead brother in her diary that she had found an unfinished story, 'The Aloe', and realized that it was what she was looking for to express her obsession with him and their shared past. In Bandol she worked at finishing the story. In April, Mansfield and Murry were tempted into moving to a grey granite cottage, Higher Tregerthen at Zennor in Cornwall, by the Lawrences, who were their immediate neighbours, but it was all more elemental than Mansfield had anticipated: 'everything seems to be made of boulders'.[22] She admits to Koteliansky that the attempt at community is a rather comic disaster:

> Frieda and I do not even speak to each other at present. Lawrence is about one million miles away, although he lives next door. He and I still speak but his voice is very faint like a voice coming over a telephone wire.[23]

Mansfield's love of domestic order and tranquillity was violated by the Lawrences' tempestuous relationship:

> I cannot discuss blood affinity to beasts for instance if I have to keep ducking to avoid the flat irons and the saucepans. And I shall *never* see sex in trees, sex in the running brooks, sex in stones & sex in everything.[24]

There is a fastidious tone of bourgeois Wellington in several of her letters from Zennor, but also a deeper anxiety about Lawrence's wish to bond with Murry, excluding Mansfield when she and Murry had just become closer than ever before. For both of them, the closeness in Bandol had partially arisen from their writing, with Mansfield absorbed in 'The Aloe' and Murry discovering the range of his critical powers in his book on Dostoevsky. At Higher Tregerthen, neither of them could write. Lawrence abhorred masks, and wanted a level of intimacy with both of them that they flinched from; they were disturbed by the freedom that Lawrence and Frieda felt to invade their domestic space. Frieda may have been misled by what she later described as Mansfield's 'terrible gift of nearness, she can come so close'.[25] Mansfield's sense of privacy was absolute. Though her gift of closeness was invaluable to her as a writer, she wrote to Ida Baker in the last year of her life: 'I am a secretive creature to my last bones.'[26] She could bear neither the Lawrences' violent rows nor the marital interaction they were able to establish after a stormy episode. Her longing for the sounds of city streets surfaced, in ironic juxtaposition to the Lawrences' debates about true sex:

> I feel about an unknown piano, my dear what certain men feel about unknown women – – No question of love – but simply 'an uncontrollable desire to stalk them' ... Not that there is even the ghost of a pianner here.[27]

However, Mansfield still felt sufficiently protective of Lawrence later in the year, accompanied by Gertler and Koteliansky, to carry off a copy of his *Amores* from people who were mocking it in the Café Royal in London; a version of the incident appears in Lawrence's *Women in Love*.

Mansfield and Murry, estranged from the Lawrences and Koteliansky, moved back to London and began to visit Lady Ottoline Morrell's house, Garsington, for week-end parties; by the winter of 1916 Mansfield had met Virginia Woolf, T. S. Eliot and Bertrand Russell. The painter, Carrington, was attracted by Mansfield's bisexual role-playing at Garsington:

> Except for Katherine I should not have enjoyed it much. But she surprised me I did not believe she would love the sort of things I do so much. Pretending to be other people & playing games & all those strange people with their intrigues ... Katherine and I wore trousers. It was wonderful being alone in the garden. Hearing the music inside, & lighted windows and feeling like two young boys – very eager.[28]

By 1917 Mansfield was absorbed by life in London and literally playing parts as she acted as an extra in a film, though an ominous undertone linking her illness and the war shadows her letters: 'my

cough is so disastrous in this Khaki weather that I can hardly con-
ceive of leaving Gower Street except feet foremost.'[29] She was also
writing plays and dialogues; she wrote a comic playlet for Christmas
1916 at Garsington, and gave a reading there of 'The Love Song of
J. Alfred Prufrock'. In April 1917 Virginia Woolf asked her for a story
for the newly established Hogarth Press; Mansfield revised 'The
Aloe' and transformed it into 'Prelude'. It did not appear until July
1918; during this time she was also publishing stories and dialogues
with the *New Age* again. 'Bliss' first appeared in August 1918 in the
English Review.

A letter written to Ottoline Morrell on 13 July 1917[30] offers an
insight into her life, when she was entering the phase on which her
reputation as a writer rests, and a few months before the nature of
her disease, which took control of her subsequent movements, was
inevitably identifiable as she began to cough up blood. The letter
expresses her awareness of the ambivalence of her feelings about
New Zealand and London, her ability to relive the past, her imaginative and analytic powers of observation. She begins by yearning for
the sea: 'But the English summer sea is not what I mean. I mean
that wild untamed water that beats about my own forlorn island.'
The hint of sentimentality is immediately pounced on by the Tiger:
'Why on earth do I call it "forlorn". My bank Manager assures me
that it's a perfect little gold mine'. The offending adjective describes
how she herself feels, though she does not say so; she tells Morrell
of unspoilt places that are not touched by commercial vulgarity in
New Zealand, but again catches herself out in self-delusion: 'I know
the most heavenly places that cannot be spoiled – and that I shall
go back to ... And I shall think of you, and wish to God I expect that
I were sitting opposite you at the Maison Lyons!'

This acknowledgement of the divided self, of fissures and disjunctions, may have been in part a reaction to Lawrence's

> conviction that the most important relationships were *not* per-
> sonal likings or intellectual agreements, but blood-commitments
> of faith and loyalty by which man could transcend the conscious
> ego, and recover truer kinds of relation than those of the modern
> wasteland.[31]

Unlike Eliot and Lawrence, she enjoys the random sounds and sensations of the city; she gives a Fauvist rather than Impressionist,

Matisse-like sketch of the lines and colour around her: 'I have some big yellow lilies in the studio. The garden door is open and the fig tree throws a wavy pattern on the floor and walls among big soft spots of sunlight.' Someone 'playing very old-fashioned dance tunes on a cheap piano' makes her 'feel the sensation of clasping young warm hands in white silk gloves'; the free play of association in the letter communicates the writer's sensuous and idly homoerotic pleasure. She then describes meeting the painter Augustus John at Margaret Morris's theatre, a club run by Fergusson's partner for dancers, painters and musicians which Mansfield often visited. The account dispenses with social interaction and homes in on a juxtaposition of the outer and the inner selves of her subjects:

> He was there with two very worn and chipped looking ladies – the saddest looking remnants of ladies – in fact they reminded me of those cups without saucers that you sometimes see outside a china shop – all-on-this-tray-one-penny. But [John] was really impressive looking. I seemed to see his mind, his haggard mind, like a strange forbidding country, full of lean sharp peaks and pools lit with a gloomy glow, and trees bent with the wind and vagrant muffled creatures tramping their vagrant way.

She is confident of her insight: 'I expect this is all rubbish, and he's really a happy man and fond of his bottle and a goo-goo eye. But I don't think so.' She modulates from witty caricature, using a sharply observed urban vignette, to an evocation of John's character through a visual impression of his mental landscape, resembling Virginia Woolf's practice in her fiction and her personal writing of using visual images for a state of mind.

In August 1917 Murry had got a job in Military Intelligence, and by November was exhausted with overwork. In her anxiety about him, Mansfield too became ill; in December she was told that she had a 'spot' in her right lung and must never winter in Britain again. In an ominous image, she says that everything she eats seems 'to go to a sort of Dead Letter Office';[32] there is no reply from the milk, cream and cheese in that she continues to lose weight. Her mother had mocked her plumpness when she was a child. Now, in a forlorn attempt to gain maternal approval, she writes to Annie Beauchamp: 'Farewell to my portliness. For I, who weighed 10 stone 3 at the age of fifteen now [at the age of 29] weigh 8 stone 6.'[33] She went alone to Bandol in January 1918; exhausted by the journey, which was prolonged and strenuous because of the war, she became ill again, and was nursed by Ida Baker who arrived, uninvited, to help her. Just before her first pulmonary haemorrhage, she is overcome by a repressed consciousness of the link between her flawed writing, seepage in the trenches and the state of her lungs. She writes to Murry that she has reread her stories and none of them are 'good enough – to march into the open (Ugh! No – I cant even in fun use these bloody comparisons. I have a horror of the way this war creeps into writing … oozes in – trickles in)'.[34] She returned to Paris but was kept there for three weeks by the prolonged bombardment by 'Big Bertha', the long-range gun that the Germans were using for shelling the city. Her enforced stay produced one of her most memorable anthropomorphic descriptions: she woke 'to hear the air *screaming*'. Sirens were the prelude to deafening gunfire, and a surreal sight:

> The whole top of a house as it were bitten out – all the windows broken – and the road of course, covered with ruin. There were trees on both sides of the street & these had just come into their new green. A great many branches were broken but on the others strange bits of clothes and paper hung. A nightdress – a chemise – a tie – they looked extraordinarily pitiful dangling in the sunny light … Two workmen arrived to clear away the debris. One found, under the dust, a woman's silk petticoat. He put it on & danced a step or two for the laughing crowd – – – That filled me with such horror that Ill never never get out of my mind the fling of his feet & his grin and the broken trees and the broken house.[35]

The cross-dressing that Carrington enjoyed with Mansfield is transformed into grotesque mockery, and the giant bite that has been taken out of the house links the cityscape to the observer's fear of being eaten rather than eating. Mansfield's identity as a confident *flâneuse* in Paris is undermined; when she was there in 1915 she wandered the streets and the parks observing the life in them:

> It was a little cafe & hideous – with a black marble top to the counter garni with lozenges of white and orange. Chauffeurs and

their wives & fat men with immense photographic apparatus sat in it – and a white fox terrier bitch – thin and eager ran among the tables.[36]

Now she was helpless, confined, and dependent on Ida Baker.

When she did get back to Britain she and Murry were married, with two painters, Brett and Fergusson, as witnesses, but Murry was preoccupied and Mansfield bitterly disappointed: 'You never once held me in your arms & called me your wife.'[37] By now weighing less than 8 stone she went to a hotel in Cornwall to be near Anne Estelle Drey and try to recover from the deterioration in her health caused by her time in Paris, but this strained her relationship with Murry. Her sleepless nights gave her an uncanny separation from herself: 'look in the glass & am frightened of that girl with burning eyes…Ill never be quite whole again'.[38] She and Murry bought a house in Hampstead in an attempt to have an ordinary married life; in a significant juxtaposition she writes of the 'house in which I do mean to express all I know about colour and form and…comfort. Fergusson is at Portsmouth; I miss him greatly.'[39] Fergusson, whose sense of colour and form had influenced her so much in the *Rhythm* days, had to report for service as a war artist; the war seemed to be closing more tightly on her life as Goodyear had died of wounds the previous year. Just as the war was ending, Mansfield's mother died in Wellington, and she was told by Dr Sorapure that her ill-health was caused originally by the gonorrhoea she had contracted in following Wilde's advice to push everything as far as it would go; she was advised to enter a sanatorium. As her symptoms proliferate and she develops neuritis, she again uses an image of eating and being eaten:

> Another New Dish – Thats the worst of illness – If one could only choose ones dish à la carte – eat it – make a grimace over it & throw the plate away – But its this infernally boring table d'hôte with all these little side dishes & kickshaws that you're simply not allowed to refuse.[40]

The horror here is also of living permanently in hotels and of having to eat to conceal that she was polluted, as the hotel authorities saw it, by tuberculosis. At Christmas she recovered sufficiently to give a party; Ida Baker remembers Mansfield looking 'almost her healthy self of younger days, wearing a rather frilly soft dress of plum-coloured silk embroidered all over with tiny bunches of flowers. It was what John Fergusson would have called "a great success".'[41]

The modernist shift in her writing during the war years takes to a more radical stage her previous Fauvist aesthetic of simplifying and paring down the form of her stories, and requiring an intuitive and imaginative response from the reader to the deep structures hinted at. She tells Murry in 1915 that she was wandering about by a quay in Paris when she recognized the shape she was aiming at for her fiction: 'Not big, almost "grotesque" in shape I mean perhaps *heavy* – – with people rather dark and seen strangely as they move in the sharp light and shadow.'[42] It seems she could be making an implicit comparison with *The Secret Sharer*; in the same letter she tells of how she was caught in the rain the previous day and offered half of an umbrella by an old man 'but as he had on a pair of tangerine coloured eye glasses I declined. I thought he was a Conrad spy.'[43] Conrad's novels and stories certainly, through their gaps and enigmas, draw the reader into providing imaginative or intuitive links, but they are heavier than Mansfield's mature fiction in that the shadows are signalled more clearly. She often refers in her personal writing at this time to a second self; sometimes it is her brother, and on one occasion she dreamt of Rupert Brooke and then spent a day with him in imagination:

> It's a game I like to play – to walk and to talk with the dead who smile and are silent, and *free*, quite finally free. When I lived alone I would often come home, put my key in the door & find someone there, waiting for me. "Hullo! Have you been here long?"[44]

The freedom belongs to her rather than the dead, in that she can construct them through her powers of mimicry as she likes, and liberate aspects of herself to interact with them.

At other times there is a much more frightening and uncanny doubling of the self, closer to *The Secret Sharer*; it appears in the *Notebooks*, and in such stories as 'Pictures', '*Je ne parle pas français*', and 'The Daughters of the Late Colonel'. A fragment in the unbound papers, probably from 1917, is a reminder of Freud's glimpse of his own reflection in 'The Uncanny':

> In the mirror she saw again that strange watchful creature who had been her companion on the journey, that woman with white cheeks and dark eyes & lips whose secret she shared, but whose air of steady desperation baffled and frightened her and seemed somehow quite out of her control.[45]

This secret self, as in *The Secret Sharer*, seems to be what Julia Kristeva, developing the implications of 'The Uncanny', calls the foreigner within, the repressed aspect of the self which emerges from the shadows to haunt the conscious mind. For Mansfield it is complicated by her increasing awareness of the foreign body within her, the bacillus, and by guilt about the young who died for others to live in the terminology of war propaganda: her brother and the thousands like him. At other times the secret self is a Fauvist beast that lurks within the self, predatory and tireless, but, like the white-faced woman, out of the control of the conscious self:

> I began thinking of all the time one has 'waited' for so many and strange people and things – the special quality it has – the *agony* of it and the strange sense that there is a second you who is outside yourself & does nothing – nothing but just listen – the other complicated you goes on – & then there is this keen – unsleeping creature – waiting to leap – It is like a dark beast – and he who comes is its prey – – –[46]

This second self is destructive rather than vulnerable, as is the sharer of Conrad's captain's cabin, who is a murderer; taboo desires, like those in 'His Sister's Keeper', find expression in Fauvist writing and painting as they do in Gauguin's pictures and in *Heart of Darkness*, where Kurtz fulfils unspeakable longings.

Though Mansfield had once warned Murry to have another literary mask ready when he removed an existing one, her attitude to this emphasis on concealment altered. In a series of letters, written just after the period focused on in this chapter but relevant for her conception of the modern, she writes to Virginia Woolf and Ottoline Morrell about her impatience with the male modernists who were her contemporaries. Having said that 'Prufrock' is a short story, she continues: '*I* don't know – These dark young men – so proud of their plumes and their black and silver cloaks and ever so expensive pompes funebres – Ive no patience.'[47] She is attacking Eliot particularly, but probably also had Ezra Pound in mind; it is a question of gender as well as modernity: 'In Joyce there is a peculiar *male* arrogance that revolts me more than I can say'.[48] Having quoted a poem of Emily Brontë's approvingly in a letter to Morrell, she says she admires its lack of disguise: 'Nowadays one of the chief reasons for ones dissatisfaction with modern poetry is one can't be sure that it really does belong to the man who writes it. It *is* so tiring – isnt it – never to leave the Masked Ball'.[49] Ruth Parkin-Gounelas sees this as a response to the impulse towards impersonality of T. S. Eliot and James Joyce. Referring to the phrase 'the man who writes it' Parkin-Gounelas observes:

> [T]he word *man* here, I think, needs to be read in a gender-specific way. Mansfield was finding her literary voice at the very time that Modernist poets – an all-male battalion headed by Ezra Pound, T. S. Eliot, and William Butler Yeats and accompanied by novelists like James Joyce and D. H. Lawrence – were formulating a poetics based on what Maud Ellman, in a recent book on the subject, calls 'scriptive self-occlusion.' While Mansfield wanted to *leave* the Masked Ball, her male contemporaries were in the thick of the revels.[50]

Though the inclusion of D. H. Lawrence in this list is questionable, the general point is persuasive. T. S. Eliot's essay on *Hamlet* published in 1919 suggests the mask-like concept of the objective correlative:

> The only way of expressing emotion in the form of art is by finding an 'objective correlative'; in other words, a set of objects, a situation, a chain of events which shall be the formula of that *particular* emotion; such that when the external facts, which must terminate in sensory experience, are given, the emotion is immediately evoked.[51]

Similarly Joyce's Stephen Dedalus in *A Portrait of the Artist as a Young Man* constructs an ideal: 'The artist, like the God of creation, remains within or behind or beyond or above his handiwork, invisible, refined out of existence, indifferent, paring his fingernails.'[52] Parkin-Gounelas's argument about the personal demonstrates that Mansfield, in her private as well as her professional writing, is 'the most ruthless critic of her own collusion with femininity. Her writing is thus a brilliant enactment but also deconstruction of the feminine code of practice'.[53] An example of her ruthless self-criticism might be the passage quoted earlier in which she writes: 'Why on earth do I call it "forlorn"', mocking the easy sentimental affectation characteristic of some feminine writing practice. At the end of this chapter her enactment of a gendered narrative voice in 'Psychology' will be considered; though the indifference of the mask is rejected, I question Parkin-Gounelas's claim that [Schreiner and] Mansfield insist upon the insertion of the author within the text, 'upon the authenticity of an authorial personality, and above all upon her direct accessibility to, or close contact with, a reading subject'.[54] The relationship between her hostility to masks and her own distrust of the personal will be explored through a discussion of 'Psychology'.

C. K. Stead, in comparing Mansfield with her contemporaries, comments on 'an indefinable all-pervasive freshness in her writing, as if every sentence had been struck off first thing on a brilliant morning'.[55] Mansfield herself says that she feels 'an infinite delight and value in *detail* – not for the sake of detail but for the life *in* the life of it'.[56] It is in her use of detail that she most resembles Lawrence as a writer. Both have an ability, unique in literary modernism in Britain, to charge natural description with such significance that the reader remembers and responds intuitively to a plant, for example the aloe in 'Prelude' and the catkin in *Women in Love*. Though the nature of the symbolic resonance is different, in that Mansfield shifts perspectives on the aloe so that it changes in different lights and as it is seen by different women, the life in the plants is almost tangible. In spite of her hostility to Lawrence's ideas about blood brotherhood, she saw in him the divinely given gift of language when he visited her in 1918:

> For me, at least, the dove brooded over him too. I loved him: He was just his old merry, rich self, laughing, describing things, giving you pictures, full of enthusiasm and joy in a future where we were all 'vagabonds' – We simply did not talk about people. We

kept to things like nuts and cowslips and fires in woods, and his black self *was* not. Oh, there is something so lovable in him – and his eagerness, his passionate eagerness for life – that is what one loves so.[57]

Lawrence's sense of exile was even stronger than Mansfield's but both felt themselves to be strangers in British artistic society, and Mansfield recognized Lawrence's violent passions, his 'black self', in herself: 'I was a deep earthy colour, & was <u>green with pinched eyes</u>. Strangely enough these fits are Lawrence and Frieda over again. I am more like L. than anybody. We are <u>unthinkably</u> alike, in fact.'[58] One of Lawrence's finest letters was written to Mansfield when he seemed most to feel that they were alike; he understood from his own experience her need to believe that she could fight her disease, and wrote about the life of the wintry landscape, the life *in* the life of it, rather than about people:

> Wonderful is to see the footmarks on the snow – beautiful ropes of rabbit prints, trailing away over the brows; heavy hare marks; a fox so sharp and dainty, going over the wall; birds with two feet that hop; very splendid straight advance of a pheasant; wood-pigeons that are clumsy and move in flocks; splendid little leaping marks of weasels, coming along like a necklace chain of berries; odd little filigree of the field-mice; the trail of a mole – it is astounding what a world of wild creatures one feels round one, on the hills in the snow.[59]

The precision of 'ropes' and 'filigree' is comparable with Mansfield's own incisive choice of metaphors, but she was intensely critical of the inadequacy of Lawrence's inept discourse in attempting to convey a woman's response to her pregnancy in *The Lost Girl*:

> Oh, don't forget where Alvina feels 'a *trill in her bowels*' and discovers herself with child. A TRILL – what does that mean – And why is it so peculiarly offensive from a man? Because it is *not on this plane* that the emotions of others are conveyed to our imagination.[60]

The accuracy with which she fastens on the flabby phrase is unerring. She feels that this novel is a betrayal of fiction in that its animality is not that of the Fauvist but of instinct without intuition and imagination:

> Lawrence denies his humanity. He denies the powers of the Imagination. He denies Life – I mean *human* life. His hero and heroine are non-human. They are animals on the prowl. They do not feel: they scarcely speak. There is not one memorable *word*. They submit to the physical response and for the rest go veiled – blind – *faceless – mindless*.[61]

If Lawrence was animalistic in Mansfield's view, Virginia Woolf was not sufficiently physical:

> [S]he has a *bird's eye* for 'that angular high stepping green insect' that she writes about [in 'Kew Gardens'] and she is not *of* her subject – she hovers over, dips, skims, makes exquisite flights – sees the lovely reflections in water that a bird must see – but *not humanly*.[62]

Mansfield reviewed the story, the outline of which she had suggested to Woolf,[63] in the *Athenaeum* with distinct ambivalence, praising it partly because it 'belongs to another age' and its 'author, with her wise smile, is as indifferent as the flowers to these odd creatures [human beings] and their ways'.[64] The implication of the review is that the story lacks engagement with the pain of its time, that the exquisite must gesture, however obliquely, to the ephemeral and mortal, though a different reading of 'Kew Gardens' could argue that it does exactly that. When Mansfield becomes a bird she does not hover and skim as Woolf does, but gets wet; she is a prosaic duck: 'When I write about ducks I swear that I am a white duck with a round eye … There follows the moment when you are *more* duck, *more* apple … than any of these objects could ever possibly be, and so you *create* them anew.' She is writing here to a painter, Brett, and her definition of the re-making of the duck by becoming it indicates how close she still is to a Fauvist aesthetic: 'I don't see how art is going to make that divine *spring* into the bounding outlines of things if it hasn't passed through the process of trying to *become* these things before recreating them'.[65]

The 'bounding' outline is relevant in both its senses to Fauvist painting: figures and objects are often outlined in a dark colour such as red, as the female figure in Fergusson's painting *Rhythm* is, but the outline is also often exuberant and vigorous, as it is both in Matisse's *La Danse* (1910) and Fergusson's *Les Eus* (1911–12). The bounding outline as demarcation line is evident in the scene in 'Prelude' in which the duck is killed: it differentiates the children, and only Kezia is separated off and appalled by the blood spilt when Pat chops off its head. She runs at him shouting 'Head back! Head back!'[66] When he picks her up to comfort her she is surprised by his ear-rings: ' " Do they come on and off?" she asked huskily' (47). The question could apply as much to the duck's head as to the ear-rings; the story partly concerns the way in which small children map the bounding outlines of things. The dynamic vigour of the outline is horribly evident in the description of the beheaded duck's posthumous progress: '[Pat] put down the body and it began to waddle – with only a long spurt of blood where the head had been; it began to pad away without a sound towards the steep bank' (46). Mansfield's writing practice, and her theory as it is expressed in the letter to Brett, are consonant with Roger Fry's explanation of the difference between Impressionism and Post-Impressionism, and the hostility of the public to what they regard as the new art's eccentricity:

> The difficulty springs from a deep-rooted conviction due to long-established custom, that the aim of painting is the descriptive imitation of natural forms. Now, these artists do not seek to give what can, after all, be but a pale reflex of actual appearance, but to arouse the conviction of a new and definite reality. They do not seek to imitate form, but to create form; not to imitate life, but to find an equivalent for life.[67]

This passage comes from his preface to the catalogue of the second Post-Impressionist Exhibition; the graphic phrase 'find an equivalent for life' describes an artistic process that can be applied to Fergusson's paintings, although Fry excluded them from his exhibition, and to 'Prelude'. Fry continues to discuss images that

> by their closely-knit unity of texture, shall appeal to our disinterested and contemplative imagination with something of the same vividness as the things of actual life appeal to our practical activities. In fact, they aim not at illusion but at reality.[68]

Art which does not imitate life but finds an equivalent for reality by
eschewing realism is what Murry gestures towards in his 'Aims and
Ideals' for the first issue of *Rhythm,* when he defines the art that the
journal will aim to present: 'Both in its pity and its brutality it shall
be real.'[69]

In 'Kew Gardens' Woolf was experimenting with a new kind of
fiction that she began when she first knew Mansfield: 'she had a
quality that I adored, and needed; I think her sharpness and reality'.[70] What she seemed to admire about Mansfield, and remembered after her death, was the bounding outline of her prose and of
her person: 'puts a line round herself completely, as Katherine
Mansfield used to wish to do, when she bought a tailor made
coat'.[71] The two writers were intensely jealous of each other but
they had a unique relationship: 'I lunched with K.M. & had 2 hours
priceless talk – priceless in the sense that to no one else can I talk in
the same disembodied way about writing; without altering my
thought more than I alter it in writing here'.[72] I have written at
length elsewhere about the significance of this friendship;[73] it had
many setbacks. Mansfield was delighted that the Woolfs published
'Prelude' but even that caused difficulties; Woolf writes to Ottoline
Morrell: 'I wish she and Murry didn't think [J. D.] Ferguson a great
artist. He has done a design for her story which makes our gorges
rise'.[74] Fergusson produced upper and lower wrappers which gender
the aloe as female. The upper wrapper shows a smiling female bust
with flame-shaped leaves curling from its shoulders, and seven
tulip-shaped flowers growing from its hair. The lower wrapper shows
a dejected female face, with drooping flowers and leaves framing it.
The designs were only used on a few copies, not surprisingly.
Though the exaggeration of the rising gorges implies that the
Woolfs were prejudiced by their friendship with Fry to be dismissive
of Fergusson, the designs restrict the fluidity of the aloe as a trope
within the story.

There were personal obstacles to the friendship between Mansfield
and Woolf, but their shared obsession with writing was a bond that
caused Woolf to observe, when she heard of Mansfield's death: 'When
I began to write, it seemed to me there was no point in writing.
Katherine won't read it ... I was jealous of her writing – the only writing I have ever been jealous of.'[75] Both were surrounded by painters
engaged in exploring the aesthetics of Post-Impressionism: Woolf's

sister was the painter Vanessa Bell, who lived with another painter, Duncan Grant, and had been married to the art critic Clive Bell, while Mansfield's closest friends were, apart from Koteliansky, Dorothy Brett, Anne Estelle Rice/Drey and J. D. Fergusson. Some of the conversations with Mansfield that Woolf records in her diary indicate that both were fascinated by formal problems comparable to those that preoccupied their artist friends, but they could refer both to life and to the structure of fiction. Woolf writes:

> I said how my own character seemed to cut out a shape like a shadow in front of me. This she understood (I give it as an example of her understanding) & proved it by telling me that she thought this bad: one ought to merge into things.[76]

Merging into things is a reminder of becoming the apple or the duck, and it implies the possibility of multiple selves, of a return to the semiotic where bounding outlines dissolve. This is neither a mask nor an authorial personality, but a recognition of the creative potential of women's experience. Though Mansfield had mimicked and worn masks, she had also lived what were apparently contradictions as Woolf had done: she had male and female lovers; she longed to be in two places, Europe and New Zealand, at once; she wanted a husband and children but was governed by the need to write professionally; she yearned for solitude and for a lively social life. She and Woolf were both complicit with patriarchy and in opposition to it. In a revealing entry in her notebook in 1918 she suggests the complexity of her relationship with her father and with patriarchy, anticipating 'The black telephone's off at the root' in Sylvia Plath's poem 'Daddy':

> I positively feel, in my hideous modern way, that I cant get into touch with my mind. I am standing gasping in one of those disgusting telephone boxes and I cant 'get through'. 'Sorry. There's no reply' tinkles out the little voice. 'Will you ring them again, exchange? A good long ring. There must be somebody there.' 'I cant get any answer.'
>
>   Then I suppose there is nobody in the building – nobody at all. Not even an old fool of a watchman. No, its dark and empty & quiet, above all – empty. Note: A queer thing is that I keep seeing it – this empty building – as my father's office. I smell it as that.

I see the cage of the clumsy wooden goods lift & the tarred ropes hanging.[77]

Mansfield and Woolf felt ashamed of their ignorance; their husbands had a classical education and degrees, and both women felt inferior and uninformed. Trying to reach her mind mechanically suggests Mansfield's anxiety about her capacity to think and reason, but she blames patriarchy for its emptiness, repeating the word 'empty' three times. She seems to feel that her father's material prosperity has left her empty-headed: that he wanted his daughters to occupy roles appropriate for the children of a successful colonial banker which did not involve much intellectual activity. The fact that she is gasping, and smells her father's office, almost hints at a link between tuberculosis and the constraints of bourgeois Wellington. The images of the cage and ropes heighten the feeling of entrapment. This is not a dream, but a waking sensation which possibly explains her interest in merging and becoming other things and people.

As Sydney Janet Kaplan interprets it:

Katherine Mansfield's aesthetics are grounded in a precocious recognition of the self as many selves – male/female being only one of several possible polarities. She had a very early experience of *multiplicity* (and I want to stress the use of this term rather than *fragmentation*, which suggests the end of a process, the breaking apart of something that was once whole...).[78]

If one accepts this terminology, *The Waste Land* suggests the end of a process, a fragmentation, whereas 'Prelude' and *To the Lighthouse* fissure into the plenitude of multiple selves. C. K. Stead observes a similarity between Eliot and Mansfield: 'the structural elements are almost always non-poetic, and are better dispensed with. This is the lesson of Pound's editorial exercise on the manuscripts of *The Waste Land*.'[79] Mansfield performed the editorial exercise herself on 'The Aloe', best seen in Vincent O'Sullivan's edition which has the texts of 'The Aloe' and of 'Prelude' on facing pages.[80] Mansfield's transformation of 'The Aloe' into 'Prelude' takes a giant bite out of it, as she says the bombing of Paris did to the city, and removes narrative explanation of the characters' psychological states; the disruption, as with the damaged city, leaves the onlooker's or reader's imagination to fill the gaps.

Mansfield, through the *New Age*, and her friendship with Lawrence and the Woolfs, was aware of Freudian theory before the war; Lawrence denounced Freudian readings of *Sons and Lovers*, and Leonard Woolf reviewed *The Psychopathology of Everyday Life* in 1914. The only time that she engages with it directly is in the self-reflexive story 'Psychology', where the topic of conversation between the two unnamed characters is whether 'the young writers of to-day – are trying simply to jump the psycho-analyst's claim?'[81] While they engage in hectic talk about this generation's awareness that it is sick, they resolutely ignore their own symptoms. Their psychological state is suggested to the reader through parapraxis, dreams, body language, repetition and indirection; the bounding outline of things has its shadow throughout the story. From the moment that the woman opens the door to the man he is curiously negated, both there and not there: ' "And you are not expecting anybody?" "Nobody at all" ' (111). The doubling is reinforced when he puts down his coat and hat 'as though he had time and to spare for everything, or as though he were taking leave of them for ever'. The two people's secret selves whisper about their pleasure in meeting, but aloud they are preoccupied with tea: she asks if he is longing for it, and he replies: 'No. Not longing.' She offers sensual, quasi-erotic, pleasures – 'short sweet almond fingers' (112) while he 'sat up, clasping his knees' as if he feels sexually threatened; he thumps an Armenian cushion and calls her 'a perfect little Chinee' (111), like a wary orientalist. She is associated with fire and with 'the lamp under its broad orange shade'; she shakes the teapot 'hot and dry over the spirit flame' (112) but he wants tea to be over and 'all these familiar things with which she lived so vividly' to be 'sent up the shadowy stairs, packed into bed and commanded to go to sleep'. Everything is reversed; the things not the people go to bed, and overtly sexual imagery is reserved for the two friends' mental intimacy: 'the special thrilling quality of their friendship was in their complete surrender. Like two open cities in the midst of some vast plain their two minds lay open to each other.' They think of themselves, in an ironic reversal, as 'eager, serious travellers, absorbed in understanding what was to be seen and discovering what was hidden' (112–13) whereas the reader realizes that the man is terrified of what might be revealed. The woman offers him the cake equivalent of Eve's apple, 'the kind of cake that might have been mentioned in the Book of Genesis' but he insists that generally food is just there to be devoured, not savoured. When he asks if this shocks her, she replies 'To the bone', again suggesting that she would yield to being devoured, but he nervously draws attention to 'that marvel of a sleeping boy's head'.

This is the crux of the story:

> It stood on the corner of the mantelpiece; the head to one side down-drooping, the lips parted, as though in his sleep the little boy listened to some sweet sound…
> 'I love that little boy,' he murmured.

(114)

This is sometimes interpreted as an indication that homoerotic feelings prevent the man from responding to the woman,[82] but the title and the sweet sound that the little boy is listening to, suggest another reading: that the boy embodies the man's desires to be left in a pre-Oedipal state of primal union with his mother, and that the man resists being woken and wants to stay in the unconscious: 'But into this unfamiliar pool the head of the little boy sleeping his timeless sleep dropped – and the ripples flowed away, away – boundlessly far – into deep glittering darkness.' The woman holds the knife which symbolizes possible severance for him: 'Carefully she cut the cake into thick little wads' (113). The word 'boundless' is repeated, juxtaposing the boy's timeless sleep with another desire that both man and woman feel: 'Again they were conscious of the boundless, questioning dark. Again, there they were – two hunters, bending over their fire, but hearing suddenly from the jungle beyond a shake of wind and a loud, questioning cry…' (115). This is the Fauvist savage within the civilized exterior; both of them are hunting, but not for the same thing. She murmurs, 'It's raining' and her voice is like his when he said 'I love that little boy.' Since rain commonly symbolizes fertility, each is indicating their deepest longing. Their intuitive response is to sustain a frenetic conversation about the novel and psychoanalysis, because what they sense is that 'their precious friendship was in danger. She was the one who would be destroyed – not they – and they'd be no party to that.' Since she is the one who signals her desire for him, and both have had sexual experiences in the past, this has nothing to do with the violation of innocence, and gestures towards his reluctance to wake from the primal sleep; earlier he looks around him 'like a man who wakes up in a train to find that he has arrived, already, at the journey's end' (114).

While they talk about psychology they are able to suppress their secret selves but then a silence falls which again opens the possibility of acknowledging their instincts:

> It was anguish – anguish for her to bear it and he would die – he'd die if it were broken … And yet he longed to break it. Not by speech. At any rate not by their ordinary maddening chatter. There was another way for them to speak to each other, and in the new way he wanted to murmur: 'Do you feel this too? Do you understand it at all?' …
>
> Instead, to his horror, he heard himself say: 'I must be off; I'm meeting Brand at six.'
>
> (116)

A murmur seems throughout the story to be the repressed voice which is shouted down by the business-like public self of both the man and the woman. The strident public voice asserts the boundaries of conventional gender roles; the man must go to a meeting and the woman hands 'him his hat and stick, smiling gaily' (116). She, the one who longed to acknowledge repressed desires, sees the beauty of the 'fall' into the night, the antithesis of the open cities on a vast plain which was the emblem of their open and honest friendship:

> She saw the beautiful fall of the steps, the dark garden ringed with glittering ivy, on the other side of the road the huge bare willows and above them the sky big and bright with stars. But of course he would see nothing of all this.
>
> (117)

What she, the Eve figure who offered the cake, sees is the dangerous allure of the fall; glittering ivy is inviting but clinging and possibly poisonous. The association of willows with love, betrayal and death, as in Desdemona's willow song and Ophelia's drowning under a willow which 'grows askant the brook',[83] confirms the woman's sense that something is over because the man, in his determination not to be roused, will not look at it. When the door-bell rings again 'an elderly virgin' stands on the doorstep offering a bunch of violets. Violets are traditionally associated with faithfulness, virginity and death, as in Wordsworth's 'Lucy', in which the narrator laments the loss of the country girl he loved: 'A violet by a mossy stone / Half hidden from the eye.' Ophelia's symbolic use of violets hints at the source of her madness; she is in love with her father's murderer who seems to have betrayed her: 'I would give you some violets, but they withered all when my father died.'[84] The woman does not immediately take the violets that are offered by the virgin, but as she stands on the door-step she and the reader have a moment of *déjà vu*:

> Again she saw the beautiful fall of the steps, the dark garden ringed with glittering ivy, the willows, the big bright sky. Again she felt the silence that was like a question. But this time she did not hesitate. She moved forward. Very softly and gently, as though fearful of making a ripple in that boundless pool of quiet, she put her arms round her friend.
>
> (118)

That this is not simply a kind gesture is clear from its effect on the elderly virgin: 'she was enfolded – more tenderly, more beautifully embraced, held by such a sweet pressure and for so long that the poor dear's mind positively reeled'. The embrace, which causes no ripple, seems an oblique response to the earlier moment at which the man dropped 'the head of the little boy sleeping his timeless sleep' causing the ripples to flow 'into deep glittering darkness'. The sexuality that the woman longed to offer the man now engulfs the virgin; as Con Coroneos observes, in Mansfield's writing violets are often associated with transgression.[85] The woman's doubling continues as she says to the virgin: 'Good night, my friend...Come again soon' and then goes in and writes in a letter to the man: 'Good night, my friend. Come again soon' (119). The orgasmic implication of the humdrum phrase now seems more relevant to the virgin than to the man.

The narrative voice in 'Psychology' moves between the man and the woman, but it specifically enacts the woman's voice, and critiques a familiar feminine code of practice. The affected tone of the voice establishes class and a gendered perspective: 'It was he, of course. And equally, of course, she oughtn't to have paid the slightest attention to it' (117). She has learned the rules of how to trap your man, just as she has learned to patronize: 'On the doorstep there stood an elderly virgin, a pathetic creature who simply idolized her (heaven knows why)' (117). The emphases are implicit, but they also indicate imprisonment; the text ironizes the social tone in the voice by gesturing towards what is repressed, the glittering ivy and the willows, and juxtaposing the social against what is unspoken. The story does not offer realism or the authenticity of an authorial personality, but rather the Fauvist juxtaposition Mansfield saw as the fictional form she aspired to in 1915, 'with people rather dark and seen strangely as they move in the sharp light and shadow'.[86]

The playful mimicry of Mansfield's early years in London was changed by her experience, particularly of the war, her brother's death, and her own precarious state of health; the barbarism that was invoked by the *Rhythm* group had become all too familiar in wartime Europe. Fauvism, with its emphasis on the savage and the outcast self, and Bergson's conception of time as heterogeneous rather than homogeneous, anticipate the breaking of boundaries that characterized the First World War. In her review of Conrad's *The Arrow of Gold* Mansfield describes the spirit of the age as 'an uneasy, disintegrating, experimental spirit'.[87] Her letters about and reviews of her contemporaries' fiction immediately after the war are ruthless in their criticism of writers who fail to respond to the disintegrating spirit, who are unchanged by the war and who, in the words of the epigraph to this chapter, have picked up the old threads as though the war had never been. She quotes dismissively from Conrad's novel a description of a *femme fatale* who listens 'as if carved six thousand years ago in order to fix for ever that something secret and obscure which is in all women'.[88] Similarly in a letter she criticizes Lawrence for a stereotypical depiction of sexuality in his protagonists: 'They submit to the physical response and for the rest go veiled – blind – *faceless* – *mindless*. This is the doctrine of mindlessness.'[89] She is dissatisfied with clichéd constructions of gender, and also, in E. M. Forster's fiction, with what she sees as English leisureliness, which precludes commitment: 'By letting himself be borne along, by welcoming any number of diversions, he can still appear to be a stranger, a wanderer, within the boundaries of his own country, and so escape from any declaration of allegiance.'[90]

In a radical shift of opinion, she writes to Sydney Schiff in 1921 saying that she now thinks she has been wrong about James Joyce because, in *A Portrait of the Artist as a Young Man,* he does not avoid declarations of allegiance:

> Some time ago I found something so repellant in his work that it was difficult to read it. It shocks me to come upon words, expressions and so on that Id shrink from in life. But now it seems to me the *new novel*, the seeking after Truth is so by far and away the most important thing that one must conquer all minor aversions. They are unworthy.[91]

Virginia Woolf remembered, at the time of Joyce's death in 1941, the beginning of Mansfield's altered attitude to Joyce's writing. In 1918 Woolf was considering the manuscript of *Ulysses* for publication by the Hogarth Press: 'One day Katherine Mansfield came, & I had it out. She began to read, ridiculing: then suddenly said, But theres some thing in this: a scene that should figure I suppose in the history of literature.'[92] What Mansfield saw in the manuscript was Molly Bloom as the 'complete complete female',[93] not a fictional stereotype, breaking the moulds that she considered Conrad and Lawrence were reverting to after the war. She was shocked that Woolf seemed, in her fiction, equally impervious to the seismic shift that, as Mansfield saw it, had occurred. She did not know that Woolf wrote *Night and Day* as a kind of formal exercise, in an attempt to avoid the mental illness that her first novel, The *Voyage Out,* caused her. In her review of *Night and Day* for the *Athenaeum* Mansfield expressed her reservations discreetly, picturing the novel as a ship coming in to harbour:

> The strangeness lies in her aloofness, her air of quiet perfection, her lack of any sign that she has made a perilous voyage – the absence of any scars... We had thought that this world was vanished for ever, that it was impossible to find on the great ocean of literature a ship that was unaware of what has been happening.[94]

The implication is of course that the writer's unawareness is culpable, and indeed she did hope to avoid scars this time. Woolf fully understood the charge: 'A decorous elderly dullard she describes me; Jane Austen up to date.'[95] What the review privately produced was a series of letters from Mansfield to Murry which contain her most revealing analysis of her own fictional techniques, and her new awareness of a kind of moral imperative for her writing. Both will be explored in the final chapter.

6
The Secret Self: January 1919 – January 1923

'We all fear when we are in waiting rooms.'[1]

'We are all sailors, bending over a great map.'[2]

'I loathe & detest shrubberies.'[3]

These contradictory alternating tropes of claustrophobia and of exploration are characteristic of Katherine Mansfield's situation and writing in the last four years of her life. She frequently confronts and writes about her fear of the presence of death in her own body; her disease traps her so that she is unable to write: 'I *am* a cough – a living, walking or lying down cough. Why I am allowed to stay in this hotel I can't imagine.'[4] The waiting room was often a literal one, as she experimented with a variety of treatments, but fearful anticipation is also woven into the texture of her letters; she even mockingly imagines heaven as a private hospital: 'If I *do* die perhaps there will be a small private heaven for consumptives only. In that case I shall see Tchekov.'[5] At the same time there is in her personal writing an exhilarated sense of freedom, and of response to new places, as when she writes to Brett about the balcony of the chalet where she lived in Switzerland: 'I always feel I am at sea – on a ship – anchored before a new, undiscovered country'.[6] Even here the whereabouts of the country is ambivalent, as the phrase 'undiscovered country' comes from Hamlet[7] for whom it is death, the destination from which no traveller returns. But her imagination seems to be liberated as her body is increasingly constrained. She persistently describes her writing in terms of travelling, and mapping out new places, both literal and psychological:

> Ive finished my new book...Ive wandered about all sorts of
> places – in and out...It is so strange to bring the dead to life
> again...And, too, one tries to go deep – to speak to the secret self
> we all have – to acknowledge that.[8]

Mansfield constantly expresses in her late fiction and in her
personal writing ideas that could stem from Bergson's emphasis
on deep structures and his analysis of time and duration, that duration is an experience of heterogeneity, the merging and becoming
process of psychic states, not of homogeneous identifiable emotions. She shows her awareness of it as a problem confronting
writers of fiction for whom one page follows another, a different
aesthetic experience for the receiver from looking at a picture and
encountering it as a whole. She writes to the novelist William
Gerhardi:

> And, yes, that is what I tried to convey in *The Garden Party* [*sic*,
> although it refers to the story rather than the volume]. The diver-
> sity of life and how we try to fit in everything, Death included.
> That is bewildering for a person of Laura's age. She feels things
> ought to happen differently. First one and then another. But life
> isn't like that. We haven't the ordering of it. Laura says, 'But all
> these things must not happen at once.' And Life answers, 'Why
> not? How are they divided from each other.' And they *do* all hap-
> pen, it is inevitable. And it seems to me there is beauty in that
> inevitability.[9]

Her first corpse and an adult party, two contradictory kinds of initiation, happen to Laura on the same day. The reader's contradictory
inference is likely to be that Laura has indeed had a revelation but it
will not alter the stultifying class structure of which she is a part,
and may not in the end change her. As Vincent O'Sullivan observes:
'Hers is a genuine moment of fulfilment, even as it does not alter in
the least the limiting rigidity of her class. The reader is directed to
acknowledge both.'[10]

Perhaps the most ironic contradiction in Mansfield's last years of
life was her full recognition of what New Zealand meant to her, at a
time when her health made it impossible for her to go there.

Fourteen of her stories written after 1918 are set in New Zealand; she writes to her father:

> [T]he longer I live the more I turn to New Zealand ... A young country is a real heritage, though it takes one time to recognise it. But New Zealand is in my very bones. What wouldn't I give to have a look at it![11]

She may have been saying what he wanted to hear, dependent as she was by then on his affection and on his financial support, but she makes similar comments in her private diaries, and records dreams: 'I was, as usual, going to N.Z.'[12] In her diary as she is writing 'At the Bay', remembering her own childhood and also revisiting the Burnell family, created first in 'Prelude', she analyses what she values about New Zealand, implicitly in comparison with England, to which she felt increasingly hostile. Her belief that art must be savage, a credo shared earlier with the *Rhythm* group and still clearly part of her aesthetic, is imaged by juxtaposing the New Zealand bush against an English garden:

> [T]he mind I love must still have wild places – a tangled orchard where dark damsons drop in the heavy grass, an overgrown little wood, the chance of a snake or two (real snakes), a pool that nobody's fathomed the depth of, and paths threaded with those little flowers planted by the wind.
>
> It must also have <u>real</u> hiding places, not artificial ones – not gazebos and mazes. And I have never yet met the cultivated mind that has not had its shrubbery. I loathe & detest shrubberies.[13]

The cultivated mind is seen as cautious and circumscribed, rather like the Botanical Gardens of her early essay, with their contrived and signposted wildernesses. She did not permit herself hiding places as far as her disease was concerned, though it is evident from her letters that she often created a mental shrubbery for Murry because she thought he needed protection from knowing the extent of her physical ordeals: 'I have tried through my illness (with one or two disastrous exceptions) to prevent him facing wholly what was happening.'[14]

The person who shared her intimacy with the disease was another colonial: Ida Baker was Rhodesian, and, with her, Mansfield was unsparing in her truthfulness. They shared their period's familiar colonial experience of repeated travel, and were both brought up to think of England as 'home' and their colony as 'out here'; in the final year of her life, when she appreciated Baker's sympathetic understanding, Mansfield writes: 'I thought for hours of the evils of uprooting. Every time one leaves anywhere something precious which ought not to be killed is left to die.'[15] Baker is the recipient of acerbic instructions relating to Mansfield's valiant attempts not to appear an invalid: 'Id rather have nothing than these ugly dull stuffs. I am a very MODERN woman. I like Life in my clothes.'[16] Almost the last entry in Mansfield's diary is a list of clothes, distinguishing between lawn, silk and crêpe de chine underwear, and itemizing the colours of her hats and dresses. The stages of Mansfield's life that have been traced in earlier chapters come poignantly together in this last phase, but throughout it she remains without self-pity. She uses her nostalgia for New Zealand without sentimentality in her stories, and her acting, mimicry and pleasure in clothes are channelled into her characters. Her instructions about her own clothes are part of a persistent colourist aesthetic; she writes to Anne Estelle Drey in 1920:

> I salute you in tangerines and the curved petals of roses thé and the crocus colour of the sea … Whenever I *examine* things here – the lovely springing line of flowers & peach leaves, par exemple, I realise what a marvellous painter you are – the beauty of your line – the *life* behind it.[17]

The emphasis on 'life' in Mansfield's personal writing, particularly at this period when she was so aware of her tenuous hold on it, signals a preoccupation that she has in common with the Post-Impressionist painters she writes to most frequently; in Roger Fry's words, quoted in the previous chapter: 'They do not seek to imitate form, but to create form; not to imitate life, but to find an equivalent for life.'[18] She was very fond of her brother-in-law, Richard, also a painter; in a letter trying to explain to him what she sees as the vital link between life and art, she moves from the colour of palm trees to life, with the implication that a painter's palette can find an equivalent for life, referring in passing to her *Rhythm* nickname, Tiger:

> Their colour is amazing. Sometimes they are bronze – sometimes gold and green – warm deep tiger-gold – & last night, under the

moon in a little window they were bright silver. And plus that the creatures are full of drawing. How marvellous life is – if only one gives oneself up to it! It seems to me that the *secret* of life is to *accept* life … People today are simply cursed by what I call the *personal*.[19]

Her letters juxtapose the wild, the Fauve, with the personal, by which she means obsessive self-analysis; she writes to another writer of fiction, Sylvia Lynd: 'One gets rather *savage* living in a little isolated villa on a wild hillside & thinking about these things. All this self examination – this fastidious probing – this hovering on the brink – its all wrong.'[20] In a letter to Murry about her reviewing she comments:

I am amazed at the sudden 'mushroom growth' of cheap psycho analysis everywhere. *Five* novels one after the other are based on it: its in everything … these people who are nuts on analysis seem to me to have *no* subconscious at all. They write to *prove* – not to tell the truth.[21]

The writer whom she continues to admire, in spite of her dislike of some of his preoccupations and of his cruelty to her, is Lawrence. Six months before her death, she read *Aaron's Rod*, and wrote about it to Koteliansky, using tropes that link the book with palms rather than with shrubberies. She acknowledges that there are aspects of it that she does not like:

They are trivial, encrusted, they cling to it as snails cling to the underside of a leaf. But apart from them there is the leaf, is the tree, firmly planted, deep thrusting, outspreading, growing grandly, alive in every twig. It is a living book; it is warm, it breathes. And it is written by a living man, with *conviction*.[22]

The book itself finds an equivalent for life, in comparison with the work of most of their contemporaries, whom she describes dismissively as 'seekers in the looking glass' who are 'half-female' and 'remind me of the greenfly in roses – they are a kind of blight'.[23] The looking glass implies contempt for surface realism, or perhaps for imaginative restriction to personal experience. 'Half-female' suggests uncertainty about gender, rather than bisexuality; in both her homosexual and heterosexual love affairs, Mansfield does not suggest that what she feels is masculine, though she played what she called a man's role in supporting Murry materially when they first met.

The catalyst for this refining of her Fauvist aesthetic of wildness, heterogeneity and commitment was her difficulty with reviewing Woolf's *Night and Day*. In her most revealing letter about her own writing, she complains initially to Murry about novelists who write as if the war has not happened. Her description of the heightening effect of the war on her vision as a writer resembles the impasto of Van Gogh's paintings, through which common things like a chair or a vase of flowers are irradiated:

> It doesn't mean that Life is the less precious of [*sic*] that the 'common things of light and day' are gone. They are not gone, they are intensified, they are illuminated. Now we know ourselves for what we are. In a way its a tragic knowledge. Its as though, even while we live again we face death. But *through Life*: thats the point. We see death in life as we see death in a flower that is fresh unfolded.[24]

Because of her illness, her tragic knowledge was particularly acute, but in this stress on the glinting ephemerality of the mortal world, and her sensuous apprehension of its transience, she characterizes her own fiction. She wants it to gesture towards death (she uses Marvell's phrase 'deserts of vast eternity') while it celebrates life, but always by hinting rather than stating:

> But the difference between you and me is (perhaps Im wrong) I couldn't tell anybody *bang out* about those deserts. They are my secret. I might write about a boy eating strawberries or a woman combing her hair on a windy morning & that is the only way I can ever mention them. But they *must* be there. Nothing less will do.[25]

This might be seen as a literary version of Bergson's influence on Fauvist painters: that different images will converge to 'direct consciousness to the precise point where there is a certain intuition to seize on'.[26] It can only happen if the writer stimulates the reader's imaginative response; Murry's 'bang out' statements, such as his self-pitying poems in *Rhythm*, annihilate speculation.

The main focus of this chapter will be on the paradox of Mansfield's final years of life: as she struggles to survive, she fluctuates between an almost religious language, including guilt and scrupulous moral analysis of her own behaviour, and the expression of an intense sense of fragmentation. Sometimes she quotes the General Confession from the *Book of Common Prayer* as when she writes: 'I have left undone those things which I ought to have done and I have done those things which I ought not to have done e.g. violent impatience with L. M. [Ida Baker].'[27] The coherence of this process of confession, repentance and amelioration is frequently stalled; later in the year she writes to Koteliansky: 'I am always conscious of this secret disruption in me.'[28] Less than a month before her death, the disruption is expressed even more emphatically, to Murry: 'You see, the question is always: *Who am I?* and until that is discovered I don't see how one can really direct anything in one's self. *Is there a Me?*'[29] The question of what identity is imbues her late stories with a thematic and formal intensity. Identity and memory become indissoluble, as reality and fiction do for the reader of her notebooks; it is often not possible to know whether one is reading a story or a passage of autobiography, in the present or the past. Returning to the past becomes a quasi-religious experience, with the boundaries between God and her father blurring into one another, on what is imaged as a sea voyage. She describes how she experiences, at night, scenes that are so vivid they seem like hallucinations:

> I lie on my right side & put my left hand up to my forehead as though I were praying. This seems to <u>induce</u> the state … People are beginning to leave the Ladies Cabin. Father puts his head in … Only there are no personalities. Neither am I there personally. People are only part of the silence, <u>not</u> of the pattern – vastly different to that – part of the <u>scheme</u>. I could always do this to a certain extent – but its only since I was really ill that this shall we call it 'consolation prize' has been given me. My God, its a marvellous thing![30]

Father on deck seems to merge into God, who is obliquely seen as the giver of the consolation prize, which is accessed through a prayerful approach. What is attained is a defeat of the personal which is itself almost godlike: 'I can call up certain persons'.[31]

Because this chapter concentrates on the relationship for her writing between Mansfield's spiritual development and her disease and death, her pervasive self-mockery and untiring sense of humour may be obscured, though this is never the case in any of her writing. Often the comedy arises from the horror of her situation, as when she is required to eat, in Switzerland, to build up her strength. She sees in the food she is offered a lack of sexual magnetism:

> And the FOOD. Its got no nerves. You know what I mean? It seems to lie down and wait for you; the very steaks are meek. Theres no contact between you and it. You're not attracted. You don't feel that keeness to meet it and know more of it and get on very intimate terms. The asparagus is always stone dead. As to the puree de pommes de terre you feel inclined to call it 'uncle'.[32]

Her macabre and brilliant punning wit plays around death: 'I told poor old L.M. yesterday that after I died to PROVE there was no immortality I would send her a coffin worm in a matchbox. She was gravely puzzled.'[33]

The beginning of 1919 brought greater financial stability than the Murrys had previously known: Mansfield's annual allowance from her father was raised to £300 and, in February, Murry was made editor of the *Athenaeum*, which enabled him to leave his job as Chief Censor at the War Office. Mansfield reviewed novels for the *Athenaeum* each week, though it remains one of the mysteries of their relationship that Murry never gave her a major literary task for the paper. In November 1919, for example, Sidney Waterlow published the leading article, 'George Eliot, 1819–1880'; Mansfield protested in a letter to Murry that he had not brought it off, and gave a tantalizing glimpse of how she could have done it herself. However she did review *Night and Day* that year, a task which was complicated by her growing friendship with Woolf. She began to feel so ill that she wrote a will in which she left all 'manuscripts note books papers letters' to Murry and asked him 'to publish as little as possible and to tear up and burn as much as possible. He will understand that I desire to leave as few traces of my camping ground as possible.'[34] The writer of a book such as this one is in no position to criticize Murry, but he clearly disregarded Mansfield's wishes in publishing her letters, journals and unfinished stories, bringing aspects of her secret self into the public arena. It is ironic to read in the published *Notebooks*: 'I don't mean that any eye but mine should read this. This is – <u>really private</u>.'[35]

Mansfield considered entering a sanatorium, but instead, on the advice of Dr Sorapure, left 'The Elephant' in Hampstead for the Mediterranean coast of Italy in September, accompanied by Ida Baker. They had to leave the hotel they first settled in because the guests complained about Mansfield's cough, and she was forced to pay to have her room disinfected; Baker writes: 'Yet another blow for Katherine, so soon after the strain of the journey: she was an outcast, an undesirable, as well as being very ill.'[36] Mansfield's relationship with Baker in these years paralleled her marriage to Murry in the extremity of its emotions, and was equally paradoxical. Mansfield herself repeatedly attacks Baker for playing hard to get: 'You're the greatest *flirt* I ever have met – a real *flirt*.'[37] She says she will not flirt back, and she is frequently maddened by what she sees as other affectations: 'Does nobody want that piece of bread & butter says L.M. You really think from her tone that she was saving the poor little darling from the river or worse, willing to adopt it as her own child.'[38] Her attacks were nearly always aimed at Baker's failures in conventional terms: that she had no lovers, no children and was not physically attractive. Mansfield depended on but resented the intimacy of their relationship, partly perhaps because of irritation that the marital role was being filled by Baker and not Murry. In a letter to Murry from the house she rented in Italy, Casetta Deerholm, she writes viciously, mocking Baker's large size: 'How I should beat her if I were married to her…I shall never shoot her because the body would be so difficult to dispose of after.'[39] Then she tells Murry that the place is made for lovers, and she longs for his arrival. Eventually, in 1922, she has the grace to acknowledge of Baker that 'I don't deserve such a wife'.[40]

Her father visited her at the Casetta Deerholm, and then returned to New Zealand and married his first wife's closest friend. In January 1920 Mansfield moved to Menton, in France, to be closer to her father's cousin, Connie Beauchamp; she wrote to Baker from there that she was to become a Roman Catholic, but did not actually do so. At about this time she reported to Murry that she had received a letter from Lawrence: 'he spat in my face & threw filth at me and said "I loathe you. You revolt me stewing in your consumption."'[41]

She returned to London in late April and stayed until mid-September, seeing Woolf for the last time and meeting her Beauchamp cousin Elizabeth, author of *Elizabeth and Her German Garden* and other fiction; Mansfield particularly admired her savage satire on patriarchy, *Vera*. Throughout the last years of her life her notebooks and letters are full of what she is reading; she comments on her contemporaries' work, but quotes most often from Shakespeare, whose plays and poetry she constantly re-read, and from Chekhov, Spenser, Coleridge, Dickens, Keats, Tolstoy and Wordsworth. She began to publish stories in the *Athenaeum*, but in December her last review appeared there, as she wanted to keep what energy she had for writing fiction. She and Ida Baker went to winter in Menton, though Mansfield was aware that her marriage was strained by repeated separations. She had to pay Sobieniowski £40 to return letters she wrote to him in 1909; this swallowed up her advance for *Bliss and Other Stories*, which was published by Constable in December.

Early in 1921 Murry left London to live with Mansfield in Menton; Ida Baker was also with them. Letters from Elizabeth Bibesco, with whom he had had some kind of flirtatious relationship, reached him there, and Mansfield replied to them, as to a badly behaved adolescent, with deflating acidity: 'I am afraid you must stop writing these little love letters to my husband while he and I live together. It is one of the things which is not done in our world.'[42] As Angela Carter says: 'She must have been formidable.'[43] In May she moved to Switzerland where there were a lot of mountain sanatoriums for tubercular patients, and doctors experimenting with cures. She and Murry settled in a chalet in the mountains near her cousin Elizabeth, and her last productive period of writing began; 'At the Bay', 'The Garden Party', 'The Voyage', 'A Married Man's Story' and 'The Doll's House' were written within three months. At the same time, she wrote a series of wonderful letters, particularly to Brett, showing an undimmed zest for landscape, and Murry's company:

> Never the same – the air like old, still wine – sounds of bells & birds and grasshoppers playing their fiddles & the wind shaking the trees. It rains & the drops in the fir trees afterwards are so flashing-bright & burning that one feels all is enchanted.[44]

Murry brought back fruits and flowers from his walks to show her, and they had a peasant maid: 'When she comes back after her afternoon out with a great bouquet of flowers and stands at the door holding them I wish Van Gogh was still alive!'[45] She was determined never to live in England again: 'Its a kind of *negation* to me and there is always a kind of silky web or net of complications spread to catch one.'[46] After over 18 months of estrangement from her father, she wrote him a letter begging for forgiveness that reads like a prayer to God the Father: '[I]t seemed to me my sin of silence was too great to beg forgiveness … I must come to you and at least acknowledge my fault … never for a moment, in my folly and my fear, have I ceased to love you and to honour you.'[47]

Their correspondence resumed, and she renewed her friendship with Orage, who was studying the teachings of Gurdjieff. Orage thought that Freud was the great analyst of the age, and what it now required was a great synthesist; Gurdjieff might be that man.[48] Mansfield also found out from Koteliansky about a Russian doctor, Manoukhin, who had conceived a scheme for curing tuberculosis by irradiating the spleen with X-rays. Murry was understandably sceptical about expensive miracle cures, but Mansfield travelled to Paris in January 1922 and took Manoukhin's extortionate and exhausting treatment for four months, during which time she was unable to write. *The Garden Party and Other Stories* was published in February. Mansfield, after a couple of unhappy months with Murry in Switzerland, with her health worse than ever, travelled to London, where she saw Orage and Koteliansky, and decided, like Orage, to risk moving in October to Gurdjieff's Institute for the Harmonious Development of Modern Man at Fontainebleau. On the last day of the year she wrote to Murry, asking him to visit her. He arrived on 9 January; on her way to her room that night she began to run upstairs, had a haemorrhage, and died. She was buried in Fontainebleau. *The Dove's Nest and Other Stories* appeared later in 1923, as did *Poems. Something Childish and Other Stories* was published in 1924.

More than any previous one, the final phase of Mansfield's life was dominated by memory. Her review of Dorothy Richardson's *The Tunnel* criticizes its hectic pace, suggesting that what it needs is memory's selection process:

> If we are to be truly alive there are large pauses in which we creep away into our caves of contemplation. And then it is, in the

silence, that Memory mounts his throne and judges all that is in our minds – appointing each his separate place, high or low, rejecting this, selecting that – putting this one to shine in the light and throwing that one into the darkness.[49]

Like other major Modernist works, such as Joyce's *A Portrait of the Artist as a Young Man*, Lawrence's *Sons and Lovers*, and Woolf's *To the Lighthouse*, Mansfield's stories are formed by memory. The difference between the function of memory, as she describes it here, and of total recall is clarified by her review of another New Zealand writer's work, Jane Mander's *The Story of a New Zealand River*. Mansfield's insistence that memory, if given the chance, highlights certain things is ignored by Mander as Mansfield demonstrates in her review. The near-quotation from St Paul, 'it profiteth us nothing',[50] is characteristic of her late writing:

> The scene is laid in the back blocks of New Zealand, and, as is almost invariably the case with novels that have a colonial setting, in spite of the fact that there is frequent allusion to the magnificent scenery, it profiteth us nothing. 'Stiff laurel-like puriris stood beside the drooping lace fringe of the lacy rimu; hard blackish kahikateas brooded over the oak-like ti-toki with its lovely scarlet berry.' What picture can that possibly convey to an English reader? What emotion can it produce? But that brings us to the fact that Miss Jane Mander is immensely hampered in her writing by her adherence to the old unnecessary technical devices – they are no more – with which she imagines it necessary to support her story.[51]

The assumption that the sentences Mansfield quotes must convey something to an *English* reader is significantly eurocentric, but of course their plodding realism and conscientious scene-setting cannot produce any emotion in a New Zealand reader either.

There is no bright Post-Impressionist light on this scene, whereas in 'At the Bay' Mansfield enables the reader to see the manuka flowers, probably unfamiliar to European readers, by shifting the narrative perspective as Linda Burnell lies idly under the manuka tree with her baby boy beside her. The fact that she looks at the flowers, and turns them rather than her son over, suggests her attitude to motherhood:

> Each pale yellow petal shone as if each was the careful work of a loving hand. The tiny tongue in the centre gave it the shape of a bell. And when you turned it over the outside was a deep bronze colour.[52]

Linda's consciousness is enacted and the unfamiliar flower is imaged; memory highlights what the reader needs to see in order to understand that the impulse that makes Linda drop off the chair on to the grass, as the manuka flowers have dropped from the tree, is her moment of flowering into love for one of her children. Bergson's analysis of the memory of crucial moments in our experience suggests that it is a complex process, not adequately represented in writing by producing a list of recalled details:

> [T]here is a third course…namely, to carry ourselves back in thought to those moments of our life when we made some serious decision, moments unique of their kind, which will never be repeated… We should see that if these past states cannot be adequately expressed in words or artificially reconstructed by a juxtaposition of simpler states, it is because in their dynamic unity and wholly qualitative multiplicity they are phases of our real and concrete duration, a heterogeneous duration and a living one.[53]

Heterogeneity is encoded in 'At the Bay' by not separating setting from action, and by using the lifting and dropping mist of the first part to hint at the moments of human rapport and misunderstanding that will follow. Experience is multiple, dynamic and contradictory: Kezia confronts the prospect of her grandmother's death and forgets it as she tickles her; Beryl longs for a demon lover and is repelled when he materializes in the garden; Linda loves and hates her husband.

Mansfield saw her own mining of her experience as an artistic resource, not a refuge; she constantly refers to it as a kind of spiritual experience, as being possessed. At the same time she expresses her own cynicism, and her wish to write 'on the subject of HATE',[54] perhaps in the interests of a scrupulous truthfulness. Although her recreation of her childhood stemmed from a yearning for the past, the savagery of that experience, as with any childhood, is revealed with ruthless lucidity, for instance in 'At the Bay' when Jonathan appears like something from *Dracula* at the window and terrifies the children. Their trust in him *is* misplaced, although they do not know it and may never find out; he dreams of abandoning his family: 'I've only one night or one day, and there's this vast dangerous garden, waiting out there, undiscovered, unexplored' (237).

Mansfield's own ability to explore the dangerous garden was increasingly frustrated by her illness. The perception from which the last stories, including 'At the Bay', arise is analysed by Mansfield herself in her *Athenaeum* review of a novel by R. O. Prowse, *A Gift of the Dusk*. The novel focuses on the macabre burgeoning of the sanatorium business of the early years of the twentieth century, following the story of the protagonist, Stephen, who discovers he is tubercular and travels to a sanatorium in Switzerland. There is a dark comedy about this terminal hotel in which the management tries to get rid of the guests just before they die to massage their success-rate statistics, and about the grim way in which the guests nevertheless try to sustain a social life. The first-person narrator analyses a situation that was familiar to the reviewer:

> Our lot is not quite the lot of the exile, and is not quite the lot of the condemned; it is the lot of the exile, and it is the lot of the condemned, but its distinctive colouring comes from the fact that it is also the lot of the outcast. We are persons who have been put away.[55]

He slowly recognizes his love for a fellow exile, Mary, whose plight must have elicited a spasm of recognition from Mansfield: 'I never pass a private house … without a little pang of envy … [My belongings] are all in my trunks … or nearly all. I am a homeless wanderer. I have a few things stored in London.'[56] What Mansfield admired about the book was the way in which it faced the situation uncompromisingly; Stephen reflects: 'The future is what one has lost. And one makes the strange discovery that, in losing it, one has lost a fundamental condition of existence.'[57] Though the novel is a kind of love story, it lacks the comfort of love scenes; the lovers are likely to cause one another a life-threatening coughing fit rather than an orgasm if they engage in fervent embraces. The conclusion is provisional, and muted; all they have is intimacy and the immediate present. Mansfield's review sees in the book a revelation of the secret self:

> It is – how shall we explain it? – as though his two selves were transposed. The self which is silent (and yet is never silent) emerges and speaks to that other self in you. It is strange to think of these ceaseless conversations that never languish or fail.[58]

What she calls 'the secret he' speaks to the reader's secret self, revealing private terrors that are usually concealed. Mansfield writes revealingly to Murry about Prowse: 'I wish I knew if he is dead … It is, after all, the only treasure heirloom we have to leave – our own little grain of truth.'[59] Her, possibly naive, assumption is that Prowse must have experienced tuberculosis to be able to describe it as he does.

The double in this passage, and increasingly in her writing, is the secret self that cannot speak; the romantic doubling of the 'world of two' that she and Murry inhabited during their happiest phase at Bandol has been fissured by separation and illness. She seems to be remembering it when, in the letter about Prowse, she writes to Murry: 'As I write I am deeply loving to you. Do you feel that? Sitting opposite to you – & talking – very quietly. You *are* there? You *do* reply? Tell me about yourself, my darling, whenever you can.'[60] Sometimes she had tried to express to him the truth she lived with: 'Once the defenses are fallen between you and Death they are not built up again. It needs such a little push – hardly that – just a false step – just not looking – and you are over.'[61] This was written in November 1919, and was the beginning of the worst crisis in her relationship with Murry, during which she rejected romantic love as a sustaining ideology. She sent Murry a series of poems which were a thinly veiled accusation that he had handed her over to death by refusing to give up everything to live with her in a climate that would prolong her life. In a brutally bouncing ballad form, with an emphatic rhyme scheme, 'The New Husband' recounts how the female narrator has been abandoned by her husband who 'would close his books and come' in six months, or perhaps a bit longer. Meanwhile she has another suitor, who is as clearly death as the mysterious lover in many of Emily Dickinson's poems:

> Said my new husband: Little dear
> It's time we were away from here

> In the road below there waits my carriage
> Ready to drive us to our marriage
> Within my home the feast is spread
> And the maids are baking the bridal bread.[62]

'Et Après' ironically celebrates the death of the sick woman, as her husband has written 'passion-fired / Poems of Sacrifice' and 'Now he's come into his own / Alone'.[63]

Murry was devastated by the poems, and replied that he was coming to join her. She wrote on the back of the letter's envelope that she had finally given up living for and by love. On the night before his arrival, she analysed what she saw as the connection between her dependent love for him and her fear of death. She believed that both had come to an end, the love because of his self-obsessed letters, and the fear of death because she had died in a dream and so was no longer afraid. In the margin she wrote later: 'important. For the confessions'.[64] One value emerges intact from the trauma: 'At the end *truth* is the one thing *worth having*: its more thrilling than love, more joyful and more passionate. It simply can*not* fail. All else fails.'[65] In this context, it is clear that she was ready to understand Prowse's novel when she read it; in a letter to Murry written as she was reviewing the book she writes, using a metaphor of exploration, about her perception not just of her own secret self but a dark doubling in creation that the healthy but deluded do not see:

> And then suffering – bodily suffering such as Ive known for three years. It has changed forever everything – even the *appearance* of the world is not the same – there is something added. *Everything has its shadow*...We resist – we are terribly frightened. The little boat enters the dark fearful gulf and our only cry is to escape – 'put me on land again'. But its useless. Nobody listens. The shadowy figure rows on. One ought to sit still and uncover ones eyes.
>
> I believe the greatest failing of all is *to be frightened*. Perfect love casteth out Fear. When I look back on my life all my mistakes have been because I was afraid...Was that why I had to look on death. Would nothing less cure me? You know, one can't help wondering, sometimes...No, not a personal God or any such nonsense. Much more likely – the soul's desperate choice...[66]

The shadowy figure can be seen as death, but also as the secret self which wants to unravel what the body knows about mortality, and not to live by fairy tales in blindness, as the letter says most people wish to do. The theme of Prowse's novel is Stephen's similar encounter with his own mortality; as he watches the dying patients around him deceiving themselves with flirtations, drink and playing social parts, he recognizes that he has been doing the same thing, and forces himself to confront his own fear honestly. In the next room to his, a woman was coughing:

> The hollow, jagged resonance of the cough itself was a torment very painful to listen to; but to try to shut one's ears would have been like a dishonouring of the bond – the bond of our common calamity. I drew the chair from the table, and just sat down and waited. To try not to be unwilling to listen, since there was nothing else one could do, looked like a point of honour.[67]

In Mansfield's words, he is sitting still and uncovering his eyes. As a result, he becomes aware of the second or secret self, what Mansfield calls the shadow and he calls the silence, which becomes familiar rather than frightening:

> It impressed me not only as very real and very near, but as very natural, very friendly, very homelike: I had a conception of it as of some other Self that was waiting to bear me company. I found I could commune with it almost as one communes with a friend.[68]

The switch as the *unheimlich* becomes *heimlich* is a willed reversal of the phenomenon Freud describes in 'The Uncanny'.

The preoccupation with doubles, which runs through Mansfield's writing from 'Summer Idylle' and 'His Sister's Keeper' on, finds its last expression in her attempts to accommodate her fear of death and to use familiarity with silence in her writing. The indirect influence of *A Gift of the Dusk* is evident in her thinking and personal writing; the novel's rather ponderously meditative style is nothing like hers, but its ruthless stripping away of self-deception and its attempt to acknowledge identification with something larger than the personal impressed her. In 1919 she suggests that if God exists, he is malign, and all humanity can do is comfort itself with stories:

> Oh, it is agony to meet corruption when one thinks all is fair – the big snail under the leaf – the spot in the childs lung – what a

WICKED WICKED God! But it is more than useless to cry out. Hanging in our little cages on the awful wall over the gulf of eternity we must sing – sing.[69]

Though she told Murry that the idea of a personal god was absurd, she wrote to Baker, in 1920 before she read Prowse's novel, saying that she was about to become a Roman Catholic because 'I knew there was a God'; she acknowledges that 'Ive always a longing to *heal* people and *make them whole*, enrich them: thats what writing means to me – to enrich – to give'.[70] A spiritual dimension becomes more insistent in her writing, although this is the only time that she seems fleetingly to opt for a specific religious faith.

The spiritual is most frequently expressed, as it is in Prowse's novel, as an imaginative effort to accept contradictions and dissolve binary oppositions, often in the attempt to become a better writer:

The mind is only the fine instrument, it's only the slave of the soul. I do agree that with a great many artists one never sees the *master*, we only know the slave. And the slave is so brilliant that he can almost make you forget the absence of the other. But one is only really *living* when one acknowledges both – or so it seems to me – and great art is achieved when the relation between these two is perfected.[71]

The effort is to recognize the shadowy presence, which is something larger than the personal, and does not concern personal immortality: 'If I lose myself in the study of life and give up *self* then I am at rest. But the more I study the religion of Christ the more I marvel at it. It seems almost impertinent to say that.'[72] She pictures her soul as a light that irradiates the capable mind, and aims for this integrated state in order to achieve what she aspires to in her writing.

Her belief in the role of the artist at this stage of her life, shadowed as it was by dying, has a moral dimension that remains consonant with the deep structures of Fauvism: 'I believe like anything in happiness and being gay and laughing but I am sure one can't afford to be less than ones *deepest self* always.'[73] As she writes about it later to Brett, she asks in the same letter whether she knows the work of the Fauvist painter Albert Marquet, as if she perceives a connection. At times the moral dimension to her letters is quite explicit, as she struggles to accept heterogeneity and its paradoxes:

> Dont think I underestimate the enormous power that parents can
> have. I dont. Its staggering – its titanic. After all they are real
> giants when we are only table high & they act according. But like
> everything else in Life – I mean all suffering, however great – we
> have to get over it...More than that and far more true is
> we have to find the *gift* in it. We cant afford to waste such an
> expenditure of feeling; we have to learn from it – and we DO, I
> most deeply believe come to be thankful for it.[74]

Her language throughout the later letters and notebooks is biblical,
with a reiterated impulse to praise a creator, although she does not
believe in one, and to refine her own behaviour by aiming at
absolute truthfulness and lack of self-deception. At the same time,
her vitriolic wit is never repressed: 'J. digs the garden as though he
were exhuming a hated body or making a hole for a loved one.'[75]

The finest expression of the spiritual impulse in her life and writing comes in an extended passage from the notebooks, written after
she had read *A Gift of the Dusk*, in which she analyses her ambition
to defeat the personal. In the first part of it, she addresses herself as
the born actress and mimic, who aims at a series of roles, each
homogeneous in itself. Her text for the meditation is 'To thine own
self be true', Polonius's advice to his son Laertes,[76] which was fash-
ionable as a quotation in the autograph books of her girlhood:

> True to oneself! Which self? Which of my many – well, really,
> thats what it looks like coming to – hundreds of selves. For what
> with complexes and suppressions, and reactions and vibrations
> and reflections – there are moments when I feel I am nothing but
> the small clerk of some hotel without a proprietor who has all his
> work cut out to enter the names and hand the keys to the wilful
> guests.[77]

Here the disrupted, fragmented self plays a series of parts but there is
no proprietor of the hotel, nothing that holds the mimicry together.
But there is an alternative possibility, and the quasi-religious impulse
towards confession is an aspect of this. The note in the margin of
her dream of dying, 'important. For the confessions', emphasizes
her attempt to prioritize honesty, although it may only be honesty

to herself, and a rejection of self-delusion:

> Is it not possible that the rage for confession, autobiography,
> especially for the memories of earliest childhood is explained
> by our persistent yet mysterious belief in a self which is continu-
> ous and permanent, which, untouched by all we acquire and
> all we shed, pushes a green spear through the leaves and
> through the mould, thrusts a sealed bud through years of dark-
> ness until, one day, the light discovers it and shakes the flower
> free and – we are alive – we are flowering for our moment upon
> the earth. This is the moment which, after all, we live for, the
> moment of direct feeling when we are most ourselves and least
> personal.[78]

This is a description of a *belief* about the self, not necessarily about
what it is: the belief that it has an organic unity which may fleetingly
be expressed. If such a moment occurs, the *personal*, obsessive self-
analysis and self-consciousness, will be irrelevant as a harmony of
mind and spirit will be achieved. In Gurdjieff's Institute Mansfield
hoped to achieve such a moment by living a life of material simplic-
ity, though the painful lists of vocabulary at the end of the notebooks
indicate what her idealism cost her: 'I am cold/bring paper to light a
fire/paper/cinders/wood/matches/flame/smoke/strong/strength/Light
a fire/No more fire/because there is no more fire'.[79]

In 1918 Mansfield wrote to Murry: 'Ive two "kick offs" in the writing game. *One* is joy ... The other ... is my old original one, and (had
I not known love) it would have been my all ... *a cry against corruption*'.[80] The alternatives are brought together as two dimensions of
the same experience, the perception that everything has its shadow,
in many of the last stories. At the same time, Mansfield's Fauvist
sense of line and form is intensified; the last letters are full of detail
about how her stories are to appear. She repeatedly tells Murry that
she must proofread her own work, that spaces must be where she
puts them: 'I cant afford mistakes. Another word wont do. I chose
every single word.'[81] She resists cuts suggested by Sadler: 'The *outline*
would be all blurred. It must have those sharp lines.'[82] She insists
that, if Murry cannot publish her stories in the *Athenaeum* as she
wrote them, he must not publish them at all. Part of the reason for
this is explained in a letter to her brother-in-law, in which she

shows how alert she still is to the Rhythmists' preoccupations:

> In Miss Brill I chose not only the length of every sentence, but
> even the sound of every sentence – I chose the rise and fall of
> every paragraph to fit her – and to fit her on that day at that very
> moment. After Id written it I read it aloud – numbers of times –
> just as one would *play over* a musical composition, trying to get it
> nearer and nearer to the expression of Miss Brill – until it fitted
> her.[83]

The heterogeneity of the arts is expressed in this; Mansfield's training as a student of the cello equips her to hear her prose. She
includes Murry in her aesthetic ambitions and wants the *Athenaeum*
to have a clear editorial and artistic line, to have '(to be 19-eleventy-
ish) GUTS'.[84]

This book concludes with a focus on two of Mansfield's last stories, both set in New Zealand, 'The Voyage' and 'A Married Man's
Story'. C. K. Stead suggests that they and 'At the Bay' overlapped
one another in the writing process, from July to September 1921,
and Alex Calder develops this proposition:

> One text nudges another. It is possible to suppose that the seventh
> section of 'At the Bay' – the one where Kezia and her grandmother
> have their conversation about death – acted as a springboard for
> 'The Voyage'; more definitely, there are echoes of 'The Voyage' in
> the narrator's reverie in the first section of 'A Married Man's Story'
> and echoes of 'A Married Man's Story' in the opening paragraph of
> the last section of 'At the Bay.'[85]

The possibility of the flowering of the self and a movement into
light, the moment when we are most ourselves and least personal, is
explored in 'The Voyage', whereas disintegration and chaotic doubling in claustrophobic darkness is the experience of the narrator of
'A Married Man's Story'. Both stories pivot on the triangle of the
mother, father and child, and in both the Post-Impressionist aesthetic of clear lines and heightened attention which discover the
significance of objects is evident.

The title of 'The Voyage' implies that the traveller is undertaking
something more significant than a trip on a ferry, and for Fenella
her short journey is a rite of passage; she is a sailor bending over a

great map. As usual in Mansfield's stories, the reader is not told how old Fenella is, but the fact that she has 'to give an undignified little skip' (321) to keep up with her father and grandmother indicates that she is a little girl, and that the perspective is hers. She clearly feels that something momentous is happening; her embarrassment as well as anguish about adult emotion are signalled when her grandmother sobs in saying goodbye to her father: 'This was so awful that Fenella quickly turned her back on them, swallowed once, twice, and frowned terribly' (323). The gentle comedy of the rhyme between her name and what she regards as her totemic object, her grandmother's umbrella, also points to a rite of passage. The 'handle, which was a swan's head, kept giving her shoulder a sharp little peck' (321); swans are not just migratory birds, but are associated in legend with transformation. When Zeus, in the form of a swan, impregnated Leda, he engendered 'The broken wall, the burning roof and tower / And Agamemnon dead' as Mansfield's contemporary, Yeats, expresses it.[86] In Hans Anderson's stories, a duckling turns into a swan, and swans transport humans between the natural and the supernatural world. In keeping with this, the Picton boat on which Fenella is sailing, carrying the swan umbrella, 'looked as if she was more ready to sail among stars than out into the cold sea' (322).

The initial atmosphere is one of death, sterility, rot and decay, implicitly seen from the child's perspective: the surroundings seem 'carved out of solid darkness', the wood-pile 'was like the stalk of a huge black mushroom' (321) and a tiny boy 'looked like a baby fly that had fallen into the cream' (322). When the reader discovers that Fenella is repressing memories of her mother's recent death, these macabre images are explained; Fenella's feeling of claustrophobia in the cabin suggests that her mother's coffin haunts her: 'What a very small cabin it was! It was like being shut up in a box with grandma' (325–6). When she looks out next morning and wonders over seeing land 'as though they had been at sea for weeks', she herself behaves like a bird, hinting at the process of transformation; she 'hopped out of her bunk' and 'stood on one leg' (328). Her perception is still funereal as she looks at 'those strange silvery withered trees that are like skeletons' and sees the houses 'like shells on the lid of a box' (328). Even when she reaches her grandparents' house with her grandmother, whose 'white waxen cheeks were blue with cold', she is haunted by death; her grandfather's voice 'sounded half stifled' (329). The gradual restoration of sensation and life is indicated through what Fenella notices; she sees a red watering-can and white flowers whose 'sweet smell was part of the cold morning' (329). Whiteness gradually becomes welcoming rather than waxen; a white cat springs up and 'Fenella buried one cold little hand in the white, warm fur, and smiled timidly' (330). The transformation is complete as 'Fenella smiled again and crooked the swan neck over the bed-rail'; something living replaces the image of the bird. She looks at her grandfather and sees, not the mechanical crane carved out of darkness that she saw at the docks, but a man called Mr Crane, whose name is that of migrant birds and who is lying in bed: 'Just his head with a white tuft and his rosy face and long silver beard showed over the quilt. He was like a very old, wide-awake bird' (330). The colourist technique modifies white from a bleached and lifeless impact on the viewer to an association with rosiness and the gleam of silver; it encodes Fenella's progress from desolation to comfort. Though a black-framed text hangs over the bed reminding the old man of his mortality, he seems to mock it in his bird-like indifference to his wife's morality: ' " Yer grandma painted that," said grandpa. And he ruffled his white tuft and looked at Fenella so merrily she almost thought he winked at her' (330). Fenella's rite of passage has been successfully negotiated, as she emerges from the darkness and can resist the gloom of the text above the bed, through the perception that her grandfather, her bird-like relative, disregards it.

'A Married Man's Story' counters the sense of completion and integrated identity in 'The Voyage' with claustrophobia and fragmentation. C. K. Stead sees it as exemplifying the Modernist principle cited earlier: '[T]he structural elements are almost always non-poetic, and are better dispensed with'. He focuses on the fact that the story is incomplete, that, in Mansfield's image of the bombed house in Paris, great bites have been taken out of it:

> In her later writing she is still learning to be content to be fragmentary, learning that it is part of the writer's job to engage the reader's imagination by leaving gaps as often as by filling them, learning not to interfere with the creative process once it has completed itself. Murry describes 'A Married Man's

Story' as 'unfinished yet somehow complete', and in that he is right.[87]

The savagery of the story is paralleled in Mansfield's work only by '*Je ne parle pas français*', also a work about a writer engaged in telling his own history. Its vicious, paradoxical and destabilizing wit is characterized by its stylistic preoccupation: the writer wants to avoid falsity and write 'just the plain truth, as only a liar can tell it' (428). It investigates the dark doubling of the self, and the fate of the Oedipalized subject, with an image from painting that literally and figuratively hangs over the whole story: '[A]s the fire quickens, falls, flares again, her shadow – an immense *Mother and Child* – is here and gone again upon the wall...' (423).

The narrator 'explains' his attitude to his wife and child by moving back into the past, where he and his mother seemed to be imprisoned by his father, a chemist; the child dreamt that 'we were living inside one of my father's big coloured bottles' (430). Curled in a foetal position, the child watched his father 'cut off at the waist by the counter', rather as he himself now appears to his wife and child with a wall of reference books in front of him: 'All the paraphernalia...of an extremely occupied man' (422). His father always appeared to him when he was a child on the staircase as a head, caught in the light from stained glass windows, 'first his bald head was scarlet, then it was yellow' (430).[88] In the child's room was a 'bust of the man called Hahnemann' (437), the founder of homeopathy. The emphasis is on male power, wielded through intellectual control, the head in evidence and everything below the waist absent or hidden. The women in the story, however, are exposed and vulnerable bodies: his mother's hands were 'pressed between her knees and my bed shook; she was shivering' (434) and the young woman who comes into the shop has been attacked, and humiliates herself further when she pays for her drink: 'her lip was cut and her eyelid looked as though it was gummed fast over the wet eye...she took the purse out of her stocking and paid him' (432). Male sexuality controls them but is concealed, horribly suggested by the objects the narrator associated with his parents as a child, 'my father's pestle and my mother's cushion' (433). The dictionary definition of 'pestle' is 'an instrument for bruising or pounding'. The narrator 'longed to be my father' (431); in wishing for this, he is expressing a desire to become lethal since 'Deadly Poison, or old D. P., was my private name for him' (435). As the title implies that the adult feels he is trapped, so reiterated tropes of imprisonment reinforce the Oedipal triangle in his childhood experience: 'I seem to have spent most of my time like a plant in a cupboard … I hide in the dark passage … listening to a silent voice inside a little cage that was me' (432–3). The child envies his father's sneering power over women; he has sexual fantasies about the battered woman, and wonders what was in his father's 'famous fivepenny pick-me-up' (431). The drink is for women, so it is perhaps not surprising that a taste of it made the narrator feel 'as though someone had given me a terrific blow on the head; I felt stunned' (431). All the women in the story behave as if they are numb and cannot control their own bodies; they are in the power of men.

The narrator uses an image that is reminiscent of Mansfield's description, in the notebooks, of the self as a hotel without a proprietor, producing a series of personae; he writes, using an even more claustrophobic image, of

> how extraordinarily *shell-like* we are as we are – little creatures, peering out of the sentry-box at the gate, ogling through our glass case at the entry, wan little servants, who can never say for certain, even, if the master is out or in …
>
> (427)

Instead of a moment of flowering, from being a wan little servant who does not know if he is part of a coherent identity, he escapes into a terrible accommodation of his second self. The way in which the second self is formulated in the story is comparable with its construction in *A Gift of the Dusk*, but it is not used to confront the terrible truths that come from acknowledging that there is no future, only the precarious present. It is also related to Bergson's idea that we have two selves, one which lives for the external world where 'we "are acted" rather than act ourselves' and the other in which we 'grasp our inner states as living things, constantly *becoming*',[89] but whereas Bergson analyses the becoming process as creative heterogeneity, for the married man it is demonic.

The first mention of the second self in the story suggests that it is a negative version of the second self that forces itself into the conscious mind in *A Gift of the Dusk*, that is, that it controls behaviour

and cannot be avoided, even when a married couple know that they
are ill-suited and should separate:

> [H]uman beings, as we know them, don't choose each other at
> all. It is the owner, the second self inhabiting them, who makes
> the choice for his own particular purposes, and – this may sound
> absurdly far-fetched – it's the second self in the other which
> responds.
>
> (427)

Within the framework of the story, this would imply that all the
women in it have second selves with a masochistic death-wish. The
narrator then pursues the nature of his own second self, and reveals
it as his room settles round him after his wife and child have left it,
taking their image on the wall with them; its 'mask is rubbed off'
and it and he broods: 'You know those stories of little children who
are suckled by wolves and accepted by the tribe, and how for ever
after they move freely among their fleet, grey brothers? Something
like that has happened to me' (428). Unlike Romulus and Remus,
however, he only realized his link with the wolves when he was adolescent, at the time when he was sexually aroused by memories of
the battered woman. He thought of her as being 'like a rat – hateful'
(436), and then had a moment of 'flowering', parallel to the
moment when 'we are most ourselves and least personal', but terrible rather than fulfilling:

> Then the shrivelled case of the bud split and fell, the plant in the
> cupboard came into flower. 'Who am I?' I thought … I saw it all,
> but not as I had seen it before … Everything lived, everything. But
> that was not all. I was equally alive and – it's the only way I can
> express it – the barriers were down between us – I had come into
> my own world!
>
> (437)

This terrible animistic universe is the result, not of confronting
death as the protagonist of *A Gift of the Dusk* does, but of allowing
the *unheimlich* to become *heimlich* in order to access what should be
forbidden parts of the self, repressed because of their violence and
cruelty. The barriers that have fallen are not between self-deception

and insight, but between restraint and savagery:

> The barriers were down. I had been all my life a little outcast; but
> until that moment no one had 'accepted' me; I had lain in the
> cupboard – or the cave forlorn. But now I was taken, I was
> accepted, claimed. I did not consciously turn away from the world
> of human beings; I had never known it; but I from that night did
> beyond words consciously turn towards my silent brothers...
>
> (437)

The fact that the story ends here, in an ellipsis, unfinished, seems
inevitable, in that the writer has been claimed by the unconscious
and so must be 'beyond words'. The cupboard he had lain in was
the domestic prison, as it is presented in the story, of the Oedipal
triangle, which replicates itself and doubles within the story. A wolf,
ominously, is more powerful than the rat-like woman, and he will
be revenged for the imaginary humiliation he has suffered.

Mansfield ended her writing career as she began it, with heterogeneous rather than homogeneous stories that melt into and permeate
one another in the reader's mind, resisting thematic or formal tidiness. One of the married man's most savage moments occurs 'when
we sat on the green bench in the Botanical Gardens and listened to
the band' (429); the urge to undermine bourgeois demarcation lines
is still as strong in the dying adult writer as it was in the girl in
Wellington. Elizabeth Bowen sees the power of Mansfield's writing
as lying in the homelessness that wearied her in her personal life,
but made her alert: 'Katherine Mansfield was saved...by two things –
her inveterate watchfulness as an artist, and a certain sturdiness
in her nature which the English at their least friendly might call
"colonial." '[90] Anne Estelle Drey, writing to Fergusson 35 years after
Mansfield's death, suggests that Mansfield's dangerous qualities have
become institutionalized; Drey attended an exhibition held at the
New Zealand High Commission in London in 1958:

> Dear Johnnie: I am enclosing a catalogue of an exhibition of
> K. M. at New Zealand House. I think you would have liked seeing
> it, very well done and very representative and it was nice meeting
> a few old friends – Richard Murry, 'the mountain' Ida Baker,
> K. M.'s two sisters. It was nostalgic to capture the long ago.[91]

But the stories, and the poems and personal writings, resist being contained as representative and keep their tantalizing power to puzzle the reader. In her recreation of 'the long ago' Mansfield creates an equivalent for life, not a museum showcase of memorabilia. Even a description of a rock pool on a remembered beach in 'At the Bay' has an almost tactile presence. Its Fauvist palette of heightened colour stimulates in the reader's awareness both a child's pleasure in exploration of the shore, and the ominous sense of the transience of that pleasure. Both on the land of the rock pool's fringe, and in the underwater, unconscious world of its depths, there is danger and entrapment as there is for the ordinary Burnell family. Now that she can no longer go to exhibitions and galleries, Mansfield's writing gives the reader the experience of looking at a dynamic picture:

> Looking down, bending over, each pool was like a lake with pink and blue houses clustered on the shores; and oh! the vast mountainous country behind those houses – the ravines, the passes, the dangerous creeks and fearful tracks that led to the water's edge. Underneath waved the sea-forest – pink thread-like trees, velvet anemones, and orange berry-spotted weeds. Now a stone on the bottom moved, rocked, and there was a glimpse of a black feeler; now a thread-like creature wavered by and was lost. Something was happening to the pink, waving trees; they were changing to a cold moonlight blue.
>
> (224)

Notes

1 Introduction

1 Scott, Margaret (ed.), *The Katherine Mansfield Notebooks* (NZ: Lincoln University Press and Daphne Brasell Associates, 1997) II, 154. All future quotations from notebooks are taken from this edition.
2 *Notebooks*, I, 1.
3 Ibid.
4 Carter, Angela, *Nothing Sacred: Selected Writings* (London: Virago, 1982) 158.
5 Hassall, Christopher, *Edward Marsh: Patron of the Arts* (London: Longmans, 1959) 226.
6 Bell, Anne Olivier and McNeillie, Andrew (eds), *The Diary of Virginia Woolf* (Harmondsworth: Penguin, 1981) II, 170–1.
7 Shaw, Helen (ed.) *Dear Lady Ginger: an exchange of letters between Lady Ottoline Morrell and D'Arcy Cresswell* (London: Century, 1984) 118.
8 Ibid.
9 Boulton, James T. and Robertson, Andrew (eds), *The Letters of D. H. Lawrence* (Cambridge University Press, 1984) III, 675.
10 Murry, Katherine Middleton, *Beloved Quixote: The Unknown Life of John Middleton Murry* (London: Souvenir Press, 1986) 35–6.
11 Gerzina, Gretchen, *Carrington: A Life of Dora Carrington 1893–1932* (London: Pimlico, 1995) 196.
12 Alpers, Antony, *The Life of Katherine Mansfield* (New York: Viking Press, 1980) 365.
13 The fifth and final volume of the *Letters* has not yet appeared.
14 *Notebooks*, I, xiii.
15 Murry, John Middleton (ed.), *Journal of Katherine Mansfield: Definitive Edition* (London: Constable, 1954) ix.
16 The comparison between Murry and Leonard Woolf is explored in Smith, Angela, *Katherine Mansfield and Virginia Woolf: A Public of Two* (Oxford: Clarendon Press, 1999) 65–9.
17 O'Sullivan, Vincent and Scott, Margaret (eds), *The Collected Letters of Katherine Mansfield* (Oxford: Clarendon Press, 1984–96) I, 318. All future quotations from the letters are taken from this edition. Punctuation, and occasionally spelling, are erratic in the letters and journals; I quote them as they appear in the text.
18 *Notebooks*, II, 125.
19 *Letters*, I, xiv.
20 *Letters*, I, 5.

151

21 *Letters*, II, 164.
22 *Letters*, II, 203.
23 Spalding, Frances, *British Art Since* 1900 (London: Thames & Hudson, 1986) 38.
24 Robins, Anna Greutzner, *Modern Art in Britain 1910–1914* (London: Merrell Holberton, 1997) 10.
25 *Letters*, IV, 42.
26 Mansfield, Katherine, *The Aloe* (London: Virago, 1985) xii.
27 Fullbrook, Kate, *Katherine Mansfield* (Brighton: Harvester, 1986) 64.
28 Robinson, Roger (ed.), *Katherine Mansfield: In from the Margin* (London: Louisiana State University Press, 1994) 73.
29 Hanson, Clare and Gurr, Andrew, *Katherine Mansfield* (London: Macmillan, 1981) 24–5.
30 *Letters*, IV, 270.
31 Martin, Wallace, *The* New Age *Under Orage: Chapters in English Cultural History* (Manchester: Manchester University Press, 1967) 143–4.
32 Bergson, Henri, *Time and Free Will: An Essay on the Immediate Data of Consciousness* (London: Swan Sonnenschein, 1910) 231–2.
33 Antliff, Mark, *Inventing Bergson: Cultural Politics and the Parisian Avant-Garde* (Princeton, NJ: Princeton University Press, 1993) 33.
34 Bergson,103–4.
35 Antliff, 48.
36 From 'Introduction to Metaphysics', quoted in Antliff, 50.
37 Antliff, 61.
38 Morris, Margaret, *The Art of J. D. Fergusson: A Biased Biography* (Glasgow: Blackie, 1974) 190.
39 Morris, 63.
40 Ibid.
41 *Rhythm*, vol. I, no. 1, Summer 1911, 12.
42 See Smith, 119–22.
43 *Rhythm* vol. I, no. 4, Spring 1912, 24.
44 *Notebooks*, II, 267.
45 Antliff, 59–60.
46 Morris, 103.
47 *Letters*, II, 35.
48 *Notebooks*, II, 133.
49 Orton, William, *The Last Romantic* (London: Cassell, 1937) 270.
50 *Diary*, II, 226.
51 Antliff, 77.
52 *Letters*, II, 56.
53 *Letters*, III, 273.
54 Hankin, C. A. (ed.), *The Letters of John Middleton Murry to Katherine Mansfield* (London: Constable, 1983) 309.
55 Mansfield, Katherine, *The Collected Short Stories* (London: Penguin, 1981) 74. All future quotations are taken from this edition.

56 Burgan, Mary, *Illness, Gender, and Writing* (London: Johns Hopkins University Press, 1994) 133–41 reads the story as homophobic.
57 Robinson, 115.
58 Alpers, Antony (ed.), *The Stories of Katherine Mansfield* (Auckland: Oxford University Press, 1984) 281.
59 *Letters*, IV, 333.

2   The Little Colonial: 1888–1908

1 O'Sullivan, Vincent (ed.), *Poems of Katherine Mansfield* (Oxford: Oxford University Press, 1988) 30.
2 Ibid.
3 *Letters*, I, 26.
4 *Poems*, x–xi.
5 *Poems*, 7.
6 *Notebooks*, I, 170.
7 *Notebooks*, I, 171.
8 Ibid.
9 Genesis 27.
10 *Notebooks*, I, 171.
11 *Letters*, I, x.
12 Berkman, Sylvia, *Katherine Mansfield: A Critical Study* (London: Geoffrey Cumberlege, Oxford University Press, 1952) 19.
13 Tomalin, Claire, *Katherine Mansfield: A Secret Life* (London: Viking, 1987) 20.
14 *Poems*, 1.
15 *Poems*, 2–3.
16 *Letters*, I, 21.
17 *Letters*, I, 44.
18 *Notebooks*, I, 81.
19 *Notebooks*, I, 150.
20 *Notebooks*, I, 110.
21 *Poems*, 18.
22 *Notebooks*, I, 108.
23 *Letters*, I, 51.
24 *Letters*, I, 61; cf. Brontë, Emily, *Wuthering Heights* (1847) vol. I, ch. 9: 'If all else perished, and *he* remained, I should still continue to be; and, if all else remained, and he were annihilated, the Universe would turn to a mighty stranger.'
25 *Notebooks*, I, 112.
26 *Notebooks*, I, 111.
27 Pater, Walter, *Miscellaneous Studies: A Series of Essays* (London: Macmillan, 1910) 178.
28 *Miscellaneous Studies*, 196.

29   Pater, Walter, *The Renaissance: Studies in Art and Poetry* (London: Macmillan, 1910) 236.
30   Ibid.
31   *Rhythm*, vol. II, July 1912, 46.
32   Symons, Arthur, *The Symbolist Movement in Literature* (London: Constable, 1908) 8–9.
33   *Notebooks*, I, 156.
34   *Notebooks*, I, 101–2; cf. Matthew 7: 24–7.
35   *Notebooks*, I, 67.
36   Alpers, *The Stories of Katherine Mansfield*, 20.
37   *Notebooks*, I, 137.
38   *Notebooks*, I, 140.
39   *Notebooks*, I, 136.
40   *Notebooks*, I, 140.
41   Ibid.
42   *Notebooks*, I, 148.
43   *Notebooks*, I, 137.
44   *Notebooks*, I, 142.
45   *Notebooks*, I, 140.
46   *Notebooks*, I, 141.
47   *Notebooks*, I, 75. Other references to the 'Idylle' are given in brackets after the quotation.
48   Kaplan, Sydney Janet, *Katherine Mansfield and the Origins of Modernist Fiction* (Ithaca, NY and London: Cornell University Press, 1991) 51.
49   [Baker, Ida], *Katherine Mansfield, the Memories of L. M.* (New York: Taplinger, 1972) 61.
50   *Notebooks*, I, 101.
51   *Notebooks*, I, 111.
52   Lawlor, P. A., *The Mystery of Maata*: *A Katherine Mansfield Novel* (Wellington: Beltane Book Bureau, 1946) 18.
53   Lawlor, 16.
54   Lawlor, 17.
55   *Notebooks*, I, 103–4.
56   *Letters*, I, 47.
57   *Letters*, I, 60.
58   *Notebooks*, I, 110.
59   Baker, 233.
60   *Collected Stories,* 520. All subsequent references are given in brackets after the quotation.
61   Ihimaera, Witi, *Dear Miss Mansfield: A Tribute to Kathleen Mansfield Beauchamp* (Auckland: Viking, 1989) 110–14.
62   Pilditch, Jan (ed.), *The Critical Response to Katherine Mansfield* (Westport, CT: Greenwood, 1996) 68.
63   Robinson, *Katherine Mansfield*, 68.
64   Murry, John Middleton (ed.), *The Letters of Katherine Mansfield* (London: Constable, 1928) II, 199.

3   A Born Actress and Mimic: August 1908 – November 1911

1 *Letters*, I, 19.
2 *Letters*, I, 50.
3 Alpers, 87.
4 *Diary*, II, 226.
5 Brophy, Brigid, *Don't Never Forget: Collected Views and Reviews* (London: Cape, 1966) 256–7.
6 Baker, *Katherine Mansfield*, 233.
7 *Letters*, I, 84.
8 Orton, 281.
9 Ibid.
10 Murry, John Middleton, *Between Two Worlds, an Autobiography* (London: Jonathan Cape, 1935) 194.
11 Tomalin, 60.
12 *Notebooks*, I, 109.
13 Tomalin, *Katherine Mansfield*, 75–8.
14 Alpers, 125.
15 *Letters*, I, 105.
16 *Letters*, I, 106–7.
17 *Letters,* I, 106.
18 Reprinted in Pilditch, 29–31.
19 Tomalin, 72.
20 Tomalin, 208.
21 *Notebooks*, I, 228. Future references to the story are taken from this text and given in brackets after the quotation.
22 Freud, Sigmund, *Art and Literature*, Pelican Freud Library, vol. 14 (Harmondsworth: Penguin Books, 1985) 371.
23 Kristeva, Julia, *Strangers to Ourselves*, trans. Leon S. Roudiez (London: Harvester Wheatsheaf, 1991) 191.
24 Genesis 4: 9.
25 Housman, A. E., *A Shropshire Lad* (1896).
26 Shakespeare, William, *King John* IV. ii. 11: 'To gild refinèd gold, to paint the lily'.
27 *Letters*, IV, 177.
28 Quoted in Martin, Wallace, *The* New Age *Under Orage: Chapters in English Cultural History* (Manchester University Press, 1967) 119, from *New Age*, VIII (8 December 1910) 135–6.
29 Martin, 176.
30 Orage, A. R., *Friedrich Nietzsche: The Dionysian Spirit of the Age* (London and Edinburgh: T. N. Foulis, 1906) 10.
31 Orage, 24.
32 Orage, 43.
33 Orage, 54–5.
34 Martin, 92.

35 *Letters*, II, 324.
36 *Poems*, 24.
37 *Letters*, I, 98.
38 Ibid.
39 *Letters*, I, 99.
40 Ibid.
41 Swinnerton, Frank, *Background with Chorus* (London: Hutchinson, 1956) 147.
42 *Letters*, II, 54.
43 *The Collected Short Stories*, 706. All future references to the stories will be given in brackets after the quotation.
44 *Letters*, III, 206.
45 *Letters*, I, 104–5.
46 Stead, C. K. (ed.), *Katherine Mansfield: Letters and Journals* (Harmondsworth: Penguin, 1977) 16.

4   The Tiger: December 1911–October 1915

1 *Notebooks*, I, 280.
2 *Poems*, 41–2.
3 Morris, *The Art of J.D. Fergusson*, 55.
4 Morris, 63.
5 *Between Two Worlds*, 134–5.
6 *Between Two Worlds*, 135.
7 *Between Two Worlds*, 154.
8 Perry, Gill, *Two Exhibitions: The Fauves, 1905, and die Brücke, 1906* (Milton Keynes: Open University Press, 1983) 20. I am indebted to my colleague Helen Beale for drawing this publication to my attention.
9 Quoted in Perry, 25.
10 Morris, 53.
11 *Between Two Worlds*, 155–6.
12 Sadler later changed his name to Sadleir, to distinguish himself from his father, also Michael Sadler, who was Chancellor of the University of Leeds and a patron of the arts.
13 Morris, 64.
14 *Rhythm*, vol. 1, no. 2 Autumn 1911, 'The Aesthetic of Benedetto Croce', 13.
15 *Colour, Rhythm and Dance: Painting and Drawings by J. D. Fergusson and His Circle in Paris* (Edinburgh: Scottish Arts Council , 1985); Sheila McGregor: 'J. D. Fergusson and the periodical "Rhythm" ', 17.
16 Pilditch, *The Critical Response to Katherine Mansfield*, 1.
17 Alpers, 135.
18 *Between Two Worlds*, 216. I have not found any further reference to the painting, and cannot identify it. Sheila McGregor, in her PhD thesis, *J. D. Fergusson: The Early Years, 1874–1918* (Courtauld Institute of Art,

May 1981), suggests of a later painting: 'One other portrait of the war years is worth mentioning, because the sitter was possibly Katherine Mansfield ... The present location of the portrait "Poise" is unknown, but Kathleen Dillon has suggested that the model could well have been Katherine Mansfield' (118). 'Poise' was reproduced in *Colour* magazine, June 1918, but Mansfield's letters and notebooks do not refer to sitting for the portrait.

19 *Letters*, I, 344.
20 *Letters*, II, 103.
21 *Colour, Rhythm and Dance*, 6.
22 Baker, *Katherine Mansfield*, 85.
23 Not four, as Sheila McGregor says in *Colour, Rhythm and Dance*, 17.
24 *Letters*, I, 125.
25 *Letters*, I, 177.
26 Lea, F. A., *The Life of John Middleton Murry* (London: Methuen, 1959) 44.
27 *Letters*, I, 198.
28 Stansky, Peter, *On or About December 1910: Early Bloomsbury and Its Intimate World* (Cambridge, MA: Harvard University Press, 1997) 216.
29 Stansky, 198–9.
30 Stansky, 199.
31 Morris, 47.
32 *Rhythm*, vol. I, no. 1, Summer 1911, 3.
33 When Stephen Swift took over as publisher the colour of the cover changed to royal blue, but the layout was otherwise unaffected.
34 Antliff, *Inventing Bergson*, 83.
35 *Rhythm*, vol. I, no. 2, Autumn 1911, 34.
36 *Colour, Rhythm and Dance*, 9.
37 Ibid.
38 This observation was made to me by my colleague, Helen Beale; though the cloven feet are not diabolical, they do counter the notion that the figure is tranquil.
39 Antliff, 99.
40 Antliff 99–100.
41 Lea, 24.
42 *Rhythm*, vol. I, no. 3, Winter 1911, 5.
43 *Rhythm*, vol. I, no. 3, Winter 1911, 17.
44 *Rhythm*, vol. II, no. 5, June 1912, 18.
45 *Rhythm*, vol. II, no. 6, July 1912, 38.
46 *Rhythm*, vol. I, no. 1, Summer 1911, 3.
47 *Rhythm*, vol. II, no. 6, July 1912, 49.
48 *Letters*, I, 124.
49 *Rhythm*, vol. I, no. 1, Summer 1911, 36.
50 *Rhythm*, vol. I, no. 2, Autumn 1911, 17.
51 *Rhythm*, vol. I, no. 2, Autumn 1911, 18.
52 *Rhythm*, vol. I, no. 2, Autumn 1911, 19.
53 *Rhythm*, vol. I, no. 3, Winter 1911, 32.

54 Kodicek, Anna (ed.), *Diaghilev Creator of the Ballets Russes* (London: Barbican Art Gallery/Lund Humphries, 1996) 90–2.
55 Buckle, Richard, *Nijinsky* (Hardmondsworth: Penguin, 1975) 280.
56 *Rhythm*, vol. II, no. 7, August 1912, 108.
57 *Rhythm*, vol. II, no. 7, August 1912, 107.
58 Ibid.
59 *Rhythm*, vol. II, no. 7, August 1912, 120.
60 *Rhythm*, vol. II, no. 9, October 1912, 224.
61 Ibid.
62 Alpers, 153.
63 *The Blue Review*, vol. I, no. 3, July 1913, 206; reprinted (London: Frank Cass, 1968).
64 *The Blue Review*, vol. I, no. 1, May 1913, 17.
65 *The Collected Short Stories*, 573. All subsequent references to the stories will be given in brackets after the quotation.
66 Pilditch, 158.
67 Dunbar, Pamela, *Radical Mansfield: Double Discourse in Katherine Mansfield's Short Stories* (London: Macmillan, 1997) 56–7.
68 Bergson, 104.
69 *Letters*, II, 14.

5 Mansfield and Modernism: November 1915– December 1918

1 *Letters*, III, 97.
2 *Letters*, II, 54.
3 *Letters*, II, 240.
4 Keegan, John, *The First World War* (London: Hutchinson, 1998) 335–6.
5 *The Somme Valley near Corbie* (1919), Australian War Memorial, Canberra.
6 Keegan, 336.
7 *Notebooks*, II, 11.
8 *Letters*, II, 82–3.
9 *Letters*, II, 14.
10 *Letters*, II, 230.
11 *Letters*, II, 283–4.
12 *Hamlet*, IV. iii. 19.
13 *Letters*, II, 339.
14 *Poems*, 54.
15 *Letters*, I, 200.
16 *Letters*, III, 216.
17 *Letters*, II, 215.
18 *Notebooks*, II, 32.
19 Raitt, Suzanne and Tate, Trudi (eds), *Women's Fiction and the Great War* (Oxford: Clarendon Press, 1997) 212.

20 O'Connor, Frank, *The Lonely Voice: A Study of the Short Story* (London: Macmillan, 1963) also sees 'Prelude' as 'an act of atonement to her brother for whatever wrong she felt she had done him, an attempt at bringing him back to life so that he and she might live forever in the world she had created for them both' (140–1).
21 *Notebooks*, II, 16.
22 *Letters*, I, 259.
23 *Letters*, I, 262.
24 *Letters*, I, 261.
25 Alpers, 218.
26 Baker, *Katherine Mansfield*, 188.
27 *Letters*, I, 265.
28 Gerzina, *Carrington*, 93.
29 *Letters*, I, 294.
30 *Letters*, I, 316–17.
31 Kinkead-Weekes, Mark, *D. H. Lawrence: Triumph to Exile 1912–1922* (Cambridge University Press, 1996) 326.
32 *Letters*, I, 357.
33 *Letters*, II, 17.
34 *Letters*, II, 70.
35 *Letters*, II, 150.
36 *Letters*, I, 157.
37 *Letters*, II, 198.
38 *Letters*, II, 230.
39 *Letters*, II, 265.
40 *Letters*, II, 286–7.
41 Baker, 130.
42 *Letters*, I, 168.
43 Ibid.
44 *Letters*, I, 186.
45 *Notebooks*, II, 113.
46 *Letters*, II, 350.
47 *Letters*, II, 318.
48 *Letters*, II, 343.
49 *Letters*, II, 334.
50 Robinson, 43.
51 Eliot, T. S., *Selected Essays* (London: Faber & Faber, 3rd edn, 1951), 'Hamlet', 145.
52 Joyce, James, *A Portrait of the Artist as a Young Man* (London: Triad/Panther, 1977) 194–5.
53 Robinson, *Katherine Mansfield*, 47.
54 Parkin-Gounelas, Ruth, *Fictions of the Female Self* (London: Macmillan, 1991) 130.
55 Stead, 19.
56 *Letters*, I, 192.
57 *Letters*, II, 284.

58   *Notebooks*, II, 143.
59   *The Letters of D. H. Lawrence*, vol. III, 328.
60   *Letters*, IV, 138.
61   Ibid.
62   *Letters*, II, 333–4.
63   See Smith, 136–40.
64   Hanson, Clare (ed.), *The Critical Writings of Katherine Mansfield* (London: Macmillan, 1987) 53–4.
65   *Letters*, I, 330.
66   *Collected Stories*, 46. All subsequent page references are given in brackets after the quotation.
67   Fry, Roger, *Vision and Design* (Harmondsworth: Pelican, 1937) 195.
68   Ibid.
69   *Rhythm*, vol. I, no. 1, Summer 1911, 36.
70   Nicholson, Nigel and Trautmann, Joanne (eds), *The Letters of Virginia Woolf*, 6 vols (London: Chatto & Windus, 1980–3) IV, 366.
71   *The Letters of Virginia Woolf*, IV, 271.
72   *The Diary of Virginia Woolf*, II, 45.
73   Smith, Angela, *Katherine Mansfield and Virginia Woolf: A Public of Two* (Oxford: Clarendon Press, 1999).
74   *The Letters of Virginia Woolf*, II, 243–4.
75   *The Diary of Virginia Woolf*, II, 226–7.
76   *The Diary of Virginia Woolf*, II, 61–2.
77   *Notebooks*, II, 134.
78   Kaplan, *Katherine Mansfield and the Origins of Modernist Fiction*, 169.
79   Pilditch, 169.
80   O'Sullivan, Vincent (ed.), *The Aloe with Prelude by Katherine Mansfield* (Wellington: Port Nicholson Press, 1982).
81   *Collected Stories*, 115.
82   Dunbar, 102: 'The man's admission of an attachment to the statue – a hint either of homosexuality or of a devotion to high aestheticism.'
83   Shakespeare, William, *Hamlet*, IV.vii.164.
84   *Hamlet*, IV.v.178. I am indebted to my colleague Nicholas Royle for suggestions on 'Psychology'.
85   Coroneos argues this in 'Flies and Violets in Katherine Mansfield', *Women's Fiction and the Great War*, 208.
86   *Letters*, I, 168.
87   Hanson, 55.
88   Hanson, 56.
89   *Letters*, IV, 138.
90   Hanson, 69–70.
91   *Letters*, IV, 352.
92   *The Diary of Virginia Woolf*, V, 353.
93   Hanson, 125.
94   Hanson, 57 and 59.
95   *Diary*, I, 314.

6 The Secret Self: January 1919 – January 1923

1 *Notebooks*, II, 287.
2 Murry, J. Middleton (ed.), *The Letters of Katherine Mansfield* (London: Constable, 1928) II, 187. Quotations from this volume will be distinguished from those in the *Collected Letters* in future by being footnoted as *Letters* (1928), followed by the page reference. All quotations are from volume II.
3 *Notebooks*, II, 163.
4 *Letters* (1928) 252.
5 *Letters*, III, 161.
6 *Letters*, IV, 317.
7 *Hamlet*, III.i.79–80.
8 *Letters*, IV, 278.
9 *Letters* (1928) 196.
10 O'Sullivan, Vincent (ed.), *Katherine Mansfield: New Zealand Stories* (Auckland: Oxford University Press, 1998) 10–11.
11 *Letters* (1928) 199.
12 *Notebooks*, II, 313.
13 *Notebooks*, II, 163.
14 *Notebooks*, II, 286.
15 *Notebooks*, II, 325.
16 *Letters*, IV, 272.
17 *Letters*, IV, 152.
18 Fry, *Vision and Design*, 195.
19 *Letters*, III, 196.
20 *Letters*, III, 199.
21 *Letters*, IV, 69.
22 *Letters* (1928) 229.
23 Ibid.
24 *Letters*, III, 97.
25 *Letters*, III, 97–8.
26 From 'Introduction to Metaphysics', quoted in Antliff, *Inventing Bergson*, 50.
27 *Notebooks*, II, 312.
28 *Letters* (1928) 260.
29 *Letters* (1928) 266.
30 *Notebooks*, II, 181.
31 Ibid.
32 *Letters*, IV, 220.
33 *Letters*, IV, 100.
34 Alpers, 366.
35 *Notebooks*, II, 280.
36 Baker, *Katherine Mansfield*, 140.
37 *Letters*, IV, 264.
38 *Notebooks*, II, 203.

39   *Letters*, III, 20.
40   *Letters* (1928) 216.
41   *Letters*, III, 209.
42   *Letters*, IV, 199.
43   Carter, *Nothing Sacred*, 160.
44   *Letters*, IV, 269.
45   *Letters*, IV, 254.
46   *Letters*, IV, 255.
47   *Letters*, IV, 307.
48   Alpers, 369.
49   Hanson, *The Critical Writings of Katherine Mansfield*, 50.
50   I Corinthians 13: 3.
51   Murry, J. Middleton (ed.), *Novels and Novelists by Katherine Mansfield* (London: Constable, 1930) 219.
52   *The Collected Short Stories*, 221. All subsequent references will be given in brackets after the quotation.
53   Bergson, *Time and Free Will*, 238–9.
54   *Notebooks*, II, 181.
55   Prowse, R. O., *A Gift of the Dusk* (London: Collins, 1920) 113.
56   Prowse, 37.
57   Prowse, 23.
58   *Novels and Novelists*, 281.
59   *Letters*, IV, 57.
60   Ibid.
61   *Letters*, III, 107.
62   *Poems*, 78.
63   Ibid.
64   *Letters*, III, 160.
65   Ibid.
66   *Letters*, IV, 75.
67   Prowse, 143.
68   Prowse, 145.
69   *Letters*, III, 37.
70   *Letters*, III, 240.
71   *Letters* (1928) 202.
72   Ibid.
73   *Letters*, III, 262.
74   *Letters*, IV, 186–7.
75   *Notebooks*, II, 158.
76   *Hamlet*, I.iii.78.
77   *Notebooks*, II, 204.
78   Ibid.
79   *Notebooks*, II, 343.
80   *Letters*, II, 54.
81   *Letters*, III, 204.
82   *Letters*, III, 273.

83 *Letters*, IV, 165.
84 *Letters*, IV, 135.
85 Robinson, *Katherine Mansfield*, 134.
86 Yeats, W. B., *The Collected Poems* (London: Macmillan, 1965), 'Leda and the Swan', 241.
87 Pilditch, *The Critical Response to Katherine Mansfield*, 169.
88 Alex Calder offers a perceptive psychoanalytic reading of this passage, and of the story, in 'My Katherine Mansfield', Robinson, 119–36.
89 Bergson, 231–2.
90 Pilditch, 74.
91 Fergusson Gallery archive 1994.813, 6 May 1958.

Bibliography

Alpers, Antony, *The Life of Katherine Mansfield* (New York: Viking Press, 1980).

Alpers, Antony (ed.), *The Stories of Katherine Mansfield* (Auckland: Oxford University Press, 1984).

Antliff, Mark, *Inventing Bergson: Cultural Politics and the Parisian Avant-Garde* (Princeton, NJ: Princeton University Press, 1993).

[Baker, Ida], *Katherine Mansfield, the Memories of L. M.* (New York: Taplinger, 1972).

Bell, Anne Olivier and McNeillie, Andrew (eds), *The Diary of Virginia Woolf*, 5 vols (Harmondsworth: Penguin, 1979–85).

Bergson, Henri, *Time and Free Will: An Essay on the Immediate Data of Consciousness* (London: Swan Sonnenschein, 1910).

Berkman, Sylvia, *Katherine Mansfield: A Critical Study* (London: Geoffrey Cumberlege, Oxford University Press, 1952.

The Blue Review, vol. I, reprinted (London: Frank Cass, 1968).

Boddy, Gillian, *Katherine Mansfield: The Woman and the Writer* (Harmondsworth: Penguin, 1988).

Boulton, James T. and Robertson, Andrew (eds), *The Letters of D. H. Lawrence*, vol. 3 (Cambridge: Cambridge University Press, 1984).

Brophy, Brigid, *Don't Never Forget: Collected Views and Reviews* (London: Cape, 1966).

Buckle, Richard, *Nijinsky* (Hardmondsworth: Penguin, 1975).

Burgan, Mary, *Illness, Gender, and Writing* (London: Johns Hopkins University Press, 1994).

Carter, Angela, *Nothing Sacred: Selected Writings* (London: Virago, 1982).

Colour, Rhythm and Dance: Painting and Drawings by J. D. Fergusson and His Circle in Paris (Edinburgh: Scottish Arts Council, 1985).

Dunbar, Pamela, *Radical Mansfield: Double Discourse in Katherine Mansfield's Short Stories* (London: Macmillan, 1997).

Eliot, T. S., Selected Essays (London: Faber & Faber, 3rd edn, 1951).

Freud, Sigmund, *Art and Literature*, Pelican Freud Library, vol. 14 (Harmondsworth: Penguin Books, 1985).

Fry, Roger, *Vision and Design* (Harmondsworth: Pelican, 1937).

Fullbrook, Kate, *Katherine Mansfield* (Brighton: Harvester, 1986).

Gerzina, Gretchen, *Carrington: A Life of Dora Carrington* 1893–1932 (London: Pimlico, 1995).

Hankin, C. A. (ed.), *The Letters of John Middleton Murry to Katherine Mansfield* (London: Constable, 1983).

Hankin, Cherry A. (ed.) *Letters between Katherine Mansfield and John Middleton Murry* (London: Virago, 1988).

Hanson, Clare (ed.), *The Critical Writings of Katherine Mansfield* (London: Macmillan, 1987).

Hanson, Clare and Gurr, Andrew, *Katherine Mansfield* (London: Macmillan, 1981).

Hassall, Christopher, *Edward Marsh: Patron of the Arts* (London: Longmans, 1959).

Ihimaera, Witi, *Dear Miss Mansfield: A Tribute to Kathleen Mansfield Beauchamp* (Auckland: Viking, 1989).

Joyce, James, *A Portrait of the Artist as a Young Man* (London: Triad/Panther, 1977).

Kaplan, Sydney Janet, *Katherine Mansfield and the Origins of Modernist Fiction* (Ithaca, NY and London: Cornell University Press, 1991).

Keegan, John, *The First World War* (London: Hutchinson, 1998).

Kinkead-Weekes, Mark, *D. H. Lawrence: Triumph to Exile 1912–1922* (Cambridge: Cambridge University Press, 1996).

Kirkpatrick, B. J., *A Bibliography of Katherine Mansfield* (Oxford: Clarendon, 1989).

Kodicek, Anna (ed.), *Diaghilev Creator of the Ballets Russes* (London: Barbican Art Gallery/Lund Humphries, 1996).

Kristeva, Julia, *Strangers to Ourselves*, trans. Leon S. Roudiez (London: Harvester Wheatsheaf, 1991).

Lawlor, P. A., *The Mystery of Maata: A Katherine Mansfield Novel* (Wellington: Beltane Book Bureau, 1946).

Lea, F. A., *The Life of John Middleton Murry* (London: Methuen, 1959).

McGregor, Sheila, *J. D. Fergusson: The Early Years, 1874–1918* (PhD thesis, Courtauld Institute of Art, May 1981).

Mansfield, Katherine, *The Collected Short Stories* (London: Penguin, 1981).

Mansfield, Katherine, *Manuscripts in the Alexander Turnbull Library* (National Library of New Zealand, 1988).

Martin, Wallace, *The* New Age *Under Orage: Chapters in English Cultural History* (Manchester: Manchester University Press, 1967).

Morris, Margaret, *The Art of J. D. Fergusson: A Biased Biography* (Glasgow: Blackie, 1974).

Murry, Katherine Middleton, *Beloved Quixote: The Unknown Life of John Middleton Murry* (London: Souvenir Press, 1986).

Murry, John Middleton (ed.), *The Letters of Katherine Mansfield* (London: Constable, 1928).

Murry, John Middleton (ed.), *Novels and Novelists by Katherine Mansfield* (London: Constable, 1930).

Murry, John Middleton, *Between Two Worlds, an Autobiography* (London: Jonathan Cape, 1935).

Murry, John Middleton (ed.), *Journal of Katherine Mansfield: Definitive Edition* (London: Constable, 1954).

Nicholson, Nigel and Trautmann, Joanne (eds), *The Letters of Virginia Woolf* 6 vols (London: Chatto & Windus, 1980–3).

O'Connor, Frank, *The Lonely Voice: A Study of the Short Story* (London: Macmillan, 1963).

Orage, A. R., *Friedrich Nietzsche: The Dionysian Spirit of the Age* (London and Edinburgh: T. N. Foulis, 1906).

Orton, William, *The Last Romantic* (London: Cassell, 1937).

O'Sullivan, Vincent (ed.), *The Aloe with Prelude by Katherine Mansfield* (Wellington: Port Nicholson Press, 1982).

O'Sullivan, Vincent (ed.), *Poems of Katherine Mansfield* (Oxford: Oxford University Press, 1988).

O'Sullivan, Vincent (ed.), *Katherine Mansfield: New Zealand Stories* (Auckland: Oxford University Press, 1998).

O'Sullivan, Vincent and Scott, Margaret (eds), *The Collected Letters of Katherine Mansfield,* 4 vols (Oxford: Clarendon Press, 1984–96).

Parkin-Gounelas, Ruth, *Fictions of the Female Self* (London: Macmillan, 1991).

Pater, Walter, *Miscellaneous Studies: A Series of Essays* (London: Macmillan, 1910).

Pater, Walter, *The Renaissance: Studies in Art and Poetry* (London: Macmillan, 1910).

Perry, Gill, *Two Exhibitions: The Fauves, 1905, and die Brücke, 1906* (Milton Keynes: Open University Press, 1983).

Pilditch, Jan (ed.), *The Critical Response to Katherine Mansfield* (Westport, CT: Greenwood, 1996).

Prowse, R. O., *A Gift of the Dusk* (London: Collins, 1920).

Raitt, Suzanne and Tate, Trudi (eds), *Women's Fiction and the Great War* (Oxford: Clarendon Press, 1997).

Rhythm vols I and II.

Robins, Anna Greutzner, *Modern Art in Britain 1910–1914* (London: Merrell Holberton, 1997).

Robinson, Roger (ed.), *Katherine Mansfield: In from the Margin* (London: Louisiana State University Press, 1994).

Scott, Margaret (ed.), *The Katherine Mansfield Notebooks* (NZ: Lincoln University Press and Daphne Brasell Associates, 1997).

Shaw, Helen (ed.), *Dear Lady Ginger: an exchange of letters between Lady Ottoline Morrell and D'Arcy Cresswell* (London: Century, 1984).

Smith, Angela, *Katherine Mansfield and Virginia Woolf: A Public of Two* (Oxford: Clarendon Press, 1999).

Spalding, Frances, *British Art Since 1900* (London: Thames & Hudson, 1986).

Stansky, Peter, *On or About December 1910: Early Bloomsbury and Its Intimate World* (Cambridge, MA: Harvard University Press, 1997).

Stead, C. K. (ed.), *Katherine Mansfield: Letters and Journals* (Harmondsworth: Penguin, 1977).

Swinnerton, Frank, *Background with Chorus* (London: Hutchinson, 1956).

Symons, Arthur, *The Symbolist Movement in Literature* (London: Constable, 1908).

Tomalin, Claire, *Katherine Mansfield: A Secret Life* (London: Viking, 1987).

Yeats, W. B., *The Collected Poems* (London: Macmillan, 1965).

Index